Luci Shaw
Christmas 1992

HORIZONS

POETRY AND TEXT BY
LUCI SHAW
CALLIGRAPHY BY
TIMOTHY R. BOTTS

HORIZONS

Exploring Creation

ZONDERVAN PUBLISHING HOUSE, GRAND RAPIDS, MICHIGAN

A Division of HarperCollins*Publishers*

HORIZONS: Exploring Creation

Copyright © 1992 by Luci Shaw and Timothy R. Botts

Requests for information should be addressed to:
Zondervan Publishing House
Grand Rapids, Michigan 49530

Library of Congress Cataloging-in-Publication Data

Shaw, Luci.
Horizons / text by Luci Shaw : design and illustrative
calligraphy by Timothy Botts
p. cm.
ISBN 0-310-57670-9
1. Meditations. I. Botts, Timothy R. II. Title.
BV4832.2.S498 1992
242—dc20   91-32997
                                                                        CIP

Unless otherwise noted, Bible quotations are paraphrased by the author.

Section title lyrics are from *I Sing the Mighty Power of God* by Isaac Watts. The fourth verse is by Luci Shaw.

Poems reprinted from *Listen to the Green*, © 1971 by Luci Shaw. Used by permission of Harold Shaw Publishers, Wheaton, IL. "Blindfold" – "But not forgotten" – "Of elms and God" – "A Song for simplicity" – "Royalty" – "Of consolation" – "Circles" – "night through a frosty window" – "forecast" – "Step on it" – "Mary's song" – "Under the snowing" – "Absolute-ly" – "The partaking" – "new birth: heart spring" – "Reluctant prophet" – "to know him risen"

Poems reprinted from *The Secret Trees*, © 1976 by Luci Shaw. Used by permission of Harold Shaw Publishers, Wheaton, IL. "The singularity of shells" – "May 20: very early morning" "... for they shall see God" – "Pneuma" – "Getting inside the miracle" – "Spring pond" – "Craftsman"

Poems reprinted from *The Sighting*, © 1981 by Luci Shaw. Used by permission of Harold Shaw Publishers, Wheaton, IL. "Judas, Peter" – "... let him hear." – "The Sighting" – "rapture" – "The foolishness of God"

Poems reprinted from *Postcard from the Shore*, © 1985 by Luci Shaw. Used by permission of Harold Shaw Publishers, Wheaton, IL. "April" – "Trauma Unit" – "Faith" – "The Omnipresence" – "Saved by optics" – "Highway song for February 14" – "... but the word of our God will stand forever" – "Epignosis" – "Some Christmas stars" – "The unveiling" – "Mixed media" – "Into orbit" – "The comforting"

Poems reprinted from *Polishing the Petoskey Stone*, © 1990 by Luci Shaw. Used by permission of Harold Shaw Publishers, Wheaton, IL. "Slide Photography: Climbing the Mount of Olives" – "Polishing the Petoskey Stone" – "Omnipotence" – "Presents" – "Sudden Valley Road" – "How to paint a promise in January" – "Quiltmaker" – "The amphibian" – "Winter chestnut: five haiku" – "Designer" – "If you care for me" – "City set on a hill"

Published in association with the literary agency of Alive Communications, P.O. Box 49068, Colorado Springs, CO 80949

Printed in Mexico

92 93 94 95 96 /   / 8 7 6 5 4 3 2 1

This edition is printed on acid-free paper and meets the American National Standards Institute Z39.48 standard.

CONTENTS

FOREWORD *by Luci Shaw*

Why did this book, *Horizons: Exploring Creation*, come to be written? Probably because, as a word-lover and a worldlover, I find myself constantly in the business of exploration, probing both inner and outer worlds, writing about realities I see, as well as some I cannot see.

New discoveries are my greatest joy, and what I continually discover is the image of the Creator printed indelibly on this, his created universe. I have always been overwhelmed by the amazing diversity of God's power in creation; his creativity never seems to duplicate itself.

A creator is a maker, an artist. Who was the first Artist? God. Since, like all of us, I am made in God's image to be a creator, my artistic mandate is to explore, to recreate, to make new, to recognize the extraordinary in the ordinary. Tim Botts, who has enriched this text with his glorious calligraphy, responds in his own unique way to the creative image of God in him, adding a whole new dimension, the visual, to the scope of this book.

We all live in a "cracked, cross-over world, waiting for bridges," bridges that will lead us from our familiar surroundings into another world of dazzling, supernatural realities. And so Tim has built some visual bridges, and I have built some word bridges for people who may not have been in the habit of reading poetry. These bridges lead from the ordinary things of life—things like quilts, and stones, and shells, and frosty windows; spiderwebs, and failure, and raspberries; hen's eggs, and accidents, and frogs—to open up the extraordinary significance of such phenomena in God's scheme of things. All of these "ordinaries" may become pointers to the holy and the beautiful if we open our inner eyes to see God at work in his world.

Listen to what the writer of *The Imitation of Christ* says: "If your heart is straight with God, then every creature will be to you a mirror of life and a book of holy doctrine." It is my hope that you will find in this book such a mirror of life, one that reflects both the Creation and its Creator.

FOREWORD *by Timothy R. Botts*

While I was studying art in college, I was privileged to get close to my professor, Arnold Bank. He exhibited a childlike wonder about everything he encountered. It was as if he were seeing our surroundings for the very first time each day.

I have been attracted to Luci Shaw's poetry for many years, because of her ability to find metaphors about God and truth in nature and everyday life. Luci has helped me to know the Creator better, to feel the benevolence of his personality and his intentions toward us. She illustrates that beauty and excellence are part of his character as reflected in his creation.

Poetry, like my expressive style of calligraphy, is an indirect way of presenting ideas. Jesus used parables. The purpose is not to obscure but to engage the mind of the audience to experience meaning on a deeper level.

Recently an art student related to me her instructor's response to the predictable nature of her work. His challenge was: "Show me something new!" The psalmist writes for us to sing a new song to the Lord. With this in mind I join Luci with my art form to celebrate our God and invite you to explore with us.

SECTION ONE

I sing the mighty power of God that made the mountains rise,
And spread the flowing seas abroad, and built the lofty skies.
I sing the wisdom that ordained the sun to rule the day;
The moon shines full at his command, and all the stars obey.

POLISHING THE PETOSKEY STONE

Petoskey Stone
(Hexagonaria)—
a fossil coral

My friend says, "Spit on it, and rub
the surface. See the pattern?"
In its hammock of lines I lift the pebble
the color of a rain cloud from the edge of the waves.
I hold it until it warms in my palm.

A week further, steering wheel in one
hand, the oval rock curved to
my other, I cradle it
a thousand miles. While we move together,
ripples across the map,
I rub its elliptical swells on my jeans,
my old sweater, these new shores of denim and wool.

The second day it starts to shine
like glycerine soap. Polished smooth,
the print rises to the surface—I see
the silk stone honeycombed with eyes
opening from a long sleep, watching me
from between the lashes of its fine spines.

Grown eons ago in a warm sea over Michigan,
buried in a long, rolling,
restless dream, now the old coral wakes
to the waves of skin, of cloth,
to the glint of the sun in my eye.

I hear someone asking: "What *is* a Petoskey stone?"

It's a fragment left over from a colony coral that grew across what is now Upper Michigan, when the land was covered by a tropical sea. Chunks of the gray fossil stone, rounded into pebbles by the action of lake waves, still show the faint hexagonal structure that characterized this coral when it was alive. The marks look like eyes of light.

This Petoskey coral, named for the small Michigan town where it was first identified, is a soft stone, easily polished with emery powder, or when rubbed on denim or woolen material. When burnished, it is semitransparent—you can see deep into it, as if to its soul, and feel that it is looking back at you.

On his birthday I gave my friend David two Petoskey stones—one "before" and one "after" polishing, with this inscription: "Can you see the difference between the rough pebble I found last week in a clutter of others at lake edge and the one I just finished polishing for you? You are a Petoskey stone, David, precious, imprinted by God with his own seeing image. First he formed you, then he chose you, when you were rough and dull, your secret beauty hidden, unsuspected. But you have gained gloss as the emery paper of criticism and conflict in God's hands has burnished you. Now your inner eyes are being opened as you see and are seen by God—a soul-recognition, a dialog of searching glances.

"Hold this polished stone in your hand and be reminded of how intricately planned you were and how splendid you are becoming. Expect the polishing to go on so that God's lovely image in you will show even more clearly."

And David said, "Now I have a new idea about what it means to be a 'living stone!'"

When I was being formed in secret,

my anatomy was not hidden from you.

As I was being woven

in the depths of the earth

your eyes saw my

  unformed body.

PSALM 139:15–16,
author's paraphrase

Hold this polished stone in your hand and be reminded of how intricately planned you were and how splendid you are becoming

13

FAITH

*Spring is a promise
in the closed fist of a long winter. All
we have got is a raw slant of light at a low
angle, a rising river of wind, and an icy rain
that drowns out green in a tide of mud. It is
the daily postponement that disillusions. (Once
again the performance has been canceled by
the management.) We live on legends
of old springs. Each evening
brings only remote possibilities of
renewal: "Maybe tomorrow." But the
evening and the morning are the umpteenth day,
and the God of sunlit Eden still looks
on the weather—and calls it good.*

Spring is a promise
IN THE CLOSED FIST

I CAN'T SEE HIM. IS HE THERE?

Perhaps it's a matter of perspective. Perhaps it's having eyes to pierce fog or dark or whatever walls us off from God. More likely, it's patience.

Disappointment is a large part of our experience with God. We live one day at a time, not knowing what will happen tomorrow. But we hope. We ache to have "the eyes of our hearts enlightened" so that we can see God, who is a Spirit. But our own efforts can never achieve it.

In the autumn of 1988, I was writer in residence at Regent College in Vancouver, Canada while living sixty-five miles south of the U.S. border. In practical terms, this meant a drive north along the coast on the days I had office hours or a class to teach. The Pacific Northwest is known for rains that fall gently but steadily for days and for clouds that hug the earth and shroud the landscape. Just a few miles in from the coast rise the Cascade Mountains and, spectacular among them, Mount Baker, when we're fortunate enough to see it!

I wrote in my journal: "For weeks I drive my highway, north in the morning, then south again at the end of the day. The mountains are on the map, but they might as well not exist, lost as they are in drizzle, fog, haze— atmospheric conditions that interfere with clear vision. Then some strong air from the Pacific sweeps away the mask, the sun shines cleanly, and Mt. Baker, towering beyond the foothills, is seen to be what it has been all along—strong, serene, unmoving, its profile cut clear against a sky of deepest blue.

"The mountains are getting whiter these days as the nights chill and snow covers their gray blue peaks. Today I kept turning my eyes from the road to glance once more at Mt. Baker, wanting to be overwhelmed again and again by the spectacular view. It is heart stopping; I can't get enough of the sight. And I can never take it for granted—I may not see it again for weeks.

"For me it's another picture of God. I mean—he's *there,* whether I see him or not. It's almost as if he's lying in wait to surprise me. And the wind is like the Spirit, sweeping away the fogs of doubt or discouragement, opening my eyes to the truth of the mountain's pure perfection, its heartbreaking beauty."

It was less like seeing than

being for the first time seen,

knocked breathless by powerful glance...

I'm still spending the power.

ANNIE DILLARD in *Pilgrim at Tinker Creek*

OF A LONG WINTER

THE SINGULARITY OF SHELLS

A shell—how small an empty space
a folding out of pink and white
a letting in of spiral light
how random? and how commonplace?

A million shells along the beach
(a million shells along the beach)
are just as fine and full of grace
as this one, here within your reach)

But lift it, hold it to your ear
and listen, surely you can hear
the swish and sigh of all the grey
and gleaming, waters, and the play
of wind with rain and sun, encased
in one small jewel box and placed
by God and oceans, in your way.

MESSAGE IN THE SAND

For all of my life, the effortless, arbitrary beauty of seaside shells and stones has signaled divine generosity. They seem to reflect the richness of God's own mind. Shells and grains of sand remind me of the importance of the microscopic and individual as well as of the vast and collective, like the endless ocean just beyond the line of lace where waves meet beach.

Some shell collectors can sit all day long in one spot on the textured banks of shells, sorting, picking through handfulls of treasures for the perfect specimen, the clearest pattern, the most intense color. The other method, which I prefer, is to walk close to the wave edges. There the wet shells can be seen individually in their tangerine and pink and butter yellow and rainbow iridescence. Their shapes draw my eye to them, as they glint in the sheen of each receding wave. They seem to whisper, "Here I am, waiting just for you." I bend and touch and rinse clean and caress each one with my eyes and my fingers before I store it in the bag I have brought along just for this. Now I can carry it home with me, to the center of a continent where there are no saltwater beaches, no shells like these.

In my home I have shells in every room—in green glass bottles on mantels or windowsills where the light can touch them. I pile shells in clay bowls together with slate pebbles and buttons of driftwood and agates and crab carapaces gleaned from all the beaches I have ever walked. Each of them seems to me to be a parable of personal choice and significance. I am amazed when I think of how God values us, bending down and raising us from among a million others, choosing us with an appreciative glint in his eye, wanting to take us home with him. God searches us out—you and me!

The LORD your God has chosen you...

to be...his treasured possession....

It was because the Lord loved you.

DEUTERONOMY 7:6,8 NRSV

In his novel *The Desert of Ice*, Jules Verne tells of a group of Arctic explorers shipwrecked in the icy wastes at the North Pole. Their lives threatened by the penetrating cold, their only resource was wood from their crushed vessel.

But how would they ignite it? Ingenuity conquered. From a polar glacier they carved a clear lens of ice. When the sun reached its zenith, they focused a beam of sunlight through the lens onto a small pile of tinder until a flame sprang up. As they fed the fire with splintered wood from the wrecked vessel, they were able to survive until they were rescued. An improbable story? The *Scientific American* thought so, until its researchers successfully duplicated the experiment. Their photo essay challenged me to write a poem:

SAVED BY OPTICS
First, they must find a chip
of cold

that has always wanted to see,
to channel the light.
Then, with hands devoid
of electricity,

without matches even,
and with only splinters
of strength left,

they must carve it out—the rough
eyeball—from under the brow
of this ice continent

and polish it between
their curved palms' last warmth
into the double convex
of a lens,

a gem without frost or crack,
cleansed by the flow
of its own tears.

Next, they must wait, shivering,
for the slow sun
to reach the zenith
of his readiness

to work with them. Now.
Focused in the eye
of ice

a matchless flame collects
until the concentrated scrutiny
of light

reads the dry tinder into
a saving kindling—ice's gift
of heat and paradox.

I had felt no compelling religious motivation to write the poem, but I soon became aware of its links with spiritual realities.

These explorers, condemned to die in the Arctic cold, came to realize they *had* a source of heat—the sun. The connection between helpless humans ("without strength" is the biblical phrase) and God, the source of light and life, was a "lens," Christ become man, *carved from the ice continent itself* (as Christ's body was made of the same stuff as ours), having "always wanted" to be a channel for light—The Incarnation! Perfect as he was, "without crack," his flame "matchless," he was human and wept with and for the rest of our race.

Images of cold and heat, light and seeing fill the poem, as does grace—the "gift" of heat. *"Now"* reminds us that "Now is the day of salvation." Jesus, God's lens through whom his love is uniquely focused, translates our splintered lives into something from which he can ignite warmth and life.

God sends trials

not because

we are strong

enough

to struggle

through them

but to help us

grow strong...

and the life

that springs up

around the edges

of endeavor

redeems

what may seem

like tragedy.

L.S.

THE SIGHTING

Out of the shame of spittle,
the scratch of dirt,
he made an anointing.

Oh, it was an agony—the gravel
in the eye, the rude slime, the brittle
clay caked on the lid.

But with the hurt
light came leaping; in the shock & shine
abstracts took flesh & flew;

winged words like view & space,
shape & shade & green & sky,
bird & horizon & sun,

turned real in a man's eye.
Thus was truth given a face
& dark dispelled & healing done.

They were young, newly married, in love. Good looking, intelligent, ambitious. Promising careers lay ahead for both of them. Though both came from Christian homes, they began to redefine "the good life," emphasizing personal fulfillment, pleasure, satisfaction, achievement, and success.

And God got left behind. Not deliberately, but subtly, gradually, their personal goals became substitutes for spiritual growth and commitment. The kingdom of God grew shadowy and insubstantial; they were growing too blind to recognize it. They were an unwitting fulfillment of Jesus' words: "With them is fulfilled the prophecy of Isaiah which says: You shall hear but not understand, and you shall see but not perceive. For their hearts have grown dull and their ears heavy of hearing and their eyes have they closed."

Closed until the day of the accident—a violent car collision in which he was badly bruised and several bones were broken, and her right leg was so badly mangled that it had to be amputated. The shock did it, forcing them to confront the realities of life and death, to recognize what is urgently important and what is merely trivial and peripheral. In the hospital recuperating, acutely grateful to be alive and together, they saw with a clearer perspective and turned in a new direction. They could see God clearly again and hear his words in their ears.

They started life over, in the service of the God who had loved them enough to shock them, to cause them the kind of pain that forced them to reexamine the issues of life. Every year, now, they mark the anniversary of the accident with a "Celebration of Life." It was for one such occasion that I wrote the poem "The Sighting."

Something like that happened to the man born blind. The therapy Jesus chose for him was anything but pleasant. Clay made of spit and gravel rubbed in his eye socket must have been stinging and disgusting. But through Jesus' fingers and voice, what really touched him was love. Imagine being able to see for the very first time. Imagine your first sight being the face of Jesus. After that, everything would look beautiful.

ONE THING I DO KNOW: I WAS BLIND, BUT NOW I SEE

JOHN 9:25, author's paraphrase

**NIGHT
THROUGH
A FROSTY
WINDOW**

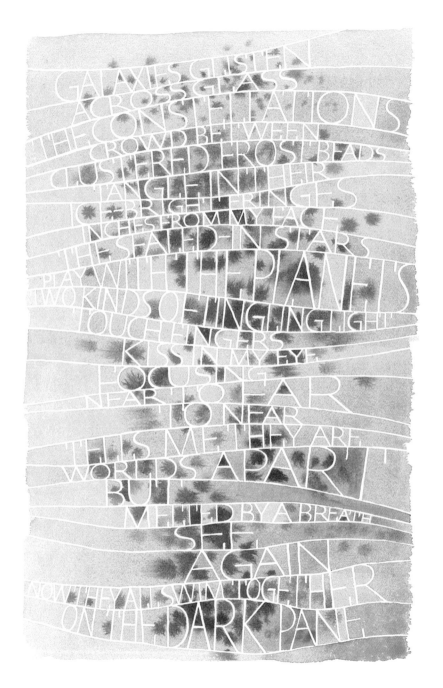

GALAXIES GLISTEN
ACROSS GLASS
THE CONSTELLATIONS
CROWD BETWEEN
CLUSTERED FROST BEADS
TANGLE IN THEIR
BRIGHT RINGS
INCHES FROM MY FACE
THESE FAR-FLUNG STARS
PLAY WITH THE PLANETS
TWO KINDS OF TINGLING LIGHT
TOUCH FINGERS
KISS IN MY EYE
FOCUSING
NEAR TO FAR
TO NEAR
THIS ME THEY ARE
WORLDS APART
BUT I
MELTED BY A BREATH
SEE
AGAIN
NOW THEY ALL SWIM TOGETHER
ON THE DARK PANE

It was one of my favorite places in our old house—the little landing halfway up the stairs. There through the evening window I could see the whole wide sky uninterrupted by streetlights or lights from other houses.

One severely cold winter all the windows in the house were decorated with flakes and scrolls of frost like a baroque patterned foil, all silver and white. That night I stood on the landing and looked out through the glass, between the stars of frost, to where, millions of light years away, the stars twinkled through space. The infinitely far stars seemed as close to my eyes as the tiny touches of frost on the glass. And when I breathed on them, lightly and warmly, they melted and melded, swimming together, the very far joined to the very near.

Years later, after photography had become my passion, I loved to record on film this aspect of the cold. The images were clearest on early mornings, with the rising sun highlighting the window frost. The marvel was that once again the far and the near, the immense and the infinitesimal, the powerful and the fragile were collaborating to create a moment of beauty and revelation for me. The sun was in service to these small frost feathers—lighting them into radiance. Is it fanciful for me to think of the sun on the frost as a metaphor of God's face shining on me, small and insignificant as I am?

When we look at your heavens...

at the stars which

you have established,

what are we humans

that you are mindful of us...

that you care for us?...

Yet you crown us

with glory and honor.

PSALM 8:3–5, author's paraphrase

MOUNTAINS

It was God's breath, blowing across
the earth's face, that first polished
the hills with wind, fired them in
the kiln of sun, exposed their
glistening flanks through scarves
of rain. Sky pointers, daily
they balanced glory on their peaks
and plateaus…

For half of every year, I live where the land is flat—prairie country stretching to the horizon, quilted in a patchwork of fields of corn, wheat, oats. But I miss the mountains, and as I travel west to the coast, its ranges—the Rockies, the Bighorns, the Cascades—seem to lift their summits like holy altars.

Mountains stand for strength; in their enormity and stability they remind us of God, who made them, who is bigger than we are and bigger than they are, who makes us look up, who has *promised* us his powerful arm to hang on to. In times when my heart sinks and I feel wholly inadequate, I imagine myself leaning into the flanks and shoulders of a towering mountain, feeling its solidity, which draws my heart even higher—to my mighty Father-Creator.

Because of their height, mountains are places of vision. From their peaks we can see clearly in any direction without interruption. We can survey the land below us like a map—the shining threads of rivers, the shapes of lakes, the deep clefts of valleys, with towns punctuating the landscape. And somehow at that height we feel there is less distance between us and God.

In the Bible mountains are often scenes of pivotal action. Think of the signs Jehovah gave on mountains: He unfurled a rainbow, a promise of life, over Ararat, where the ark unloaded its precious cargo after the Flood. On Sinai he ignited a bush as a sign to Moses of his unquenchable presence. Many years later, on the same mountain, Moses received from the hands of the Almighty the two tablets of stone engraved with God's standards for human conduct. And on Mount Carmel

God unleashed a power unmatched by the pagan baals as he kindled Elijah's water-soaked sacrifice into flame.

On Mount Moriah Isaac was bound on an altar by his father, Abraham, in obedience to God, but was saved from slaughter when a ram was divinely provided as a substitute sacrifice. It was on the same mountain—Moriah—that the Lord "broke forth" on Uzzah for his brashness in touching the sacred ark of the covenant. And there he blessed Obed-Edom for secluding the ark in his threshing floor, the very spot where Solomon eventually built the temple as God's house on earth.

And finally, the focal event of all time, which gave meaning to all the others, was enacted there:

Time and the Spirit…
focus our seeing on
slain Son/sacrificial Lamb (displayed now
as a whole world's ransom) on the one
out-thrusting rind of rock—Moriah,
Zion, Golgotha, Skull Hill—showplace
for God at work.

I WILL LIFT MY EYES TO THE MOUNTAINS. FROM WHERE DOES MY TRUE HELP COMETH? FROM THE LORD, WHO MADE HEAVEN AND EARTH

PSALM 121:1–2, author's paraphrase

**GETTING
INSIDE THE
MIRACLE**

*No. He is too quick. We never
catch him at it. He is there
sooner than our thought or prayer.
Searching backwards
we cannot discover how
or get inside the miracle.*

*Even if it were here and now
how would we describe the just-born trees
swimming into place at their green creation,
flowering upward in the air
with all their thin twigs quivering
in the gusts of grace? or the great
white whales fluking through crystalline seas
like recently-inflated balloons? Who could
time the beat of the man's heart
as the woman comes close enough to mend
his newly-hollow side? Who will
diagram the gynecology
of incarnation, the trigonometry of trinity?
or chemically analyze wine
from a well? Will anyone stand beside
the moving stone, and plot the bright
trajectory of the ascension, and explain
the tongues of fire
telling both heat and light?*

It is the glory of God to conceal a matter

PROVERBS 25:2

I am marvelling, as I drive south along the coastal highway, at the drama of landscape—the swift changes. First the hills are brooding profiles against the virgin sky. Then the light shifts, clouds rest on the crests, the valleys become brilliant murals of color that turn the rain-heavy clouds to menace.

The whole thing is solvent. I am entranced by its transience. l find a place to park, but by the time I turn off the ignition, take camera from case, and emerge from my car to frame and focus what has reached out and touched my heart through my eyes, it has gone dull, and the light anoints the opposite side of the valley. It is impossible to predict where the sun will touch down next.

And I am just as fickle, or God is moving too fast for me to catch him. But I can't help myself. I keep watching, waiting, taking off after where I think his brightness is about to blaze.

**ELEUTHERA ISLAND,
BAHAMAS**

*Finned, masked, body bright as a bone under
water, traced with tricks of waves' edges,
I have left land to shift into new gear. It is
like flying—weightless, floating. Thighs
slick as a seal's sides, I fluke through
colored schools of fish that turn at a flick,
glint past my foreign cheek. Or I can hang
motionless in the caves of light, clear as air.
My hands, down-branched like sea-stalks, touch
at a coral's rasp and the pink weeds' slip and frill.*

*Having swum like a gull, I long now
to crease the sea's skin, to break water,
to rise airborne, to fly, gliding easy as a fish,
to clothe bird bones, wings angled
flat as planes, plucked high, dripping,
by the lift of feathers, the balance of beak
and body, the up-trusting eye—Oh
to be at home in the sea, and as clean
and careless, there in the fathomless sky!*

One of our natural human restrictions is that we are land bound, tied to *terra firma*. Submarines and space craft show our strenuous efforts to extend our boundaries. But they are at best artificial. We are still bipeds; we haven't grown fins or wings.

On holiday in the Bahamian island of Eleuthera (whose very name means freedom in Greek), I sampled what it might *feel* like to be free. It was snorkeling that gave me the dreamlike experience of floating on the surface, equipped only with face mask, breathing tube, and flippers. The poem tells it—the release from gravity, the buoyancy of the clear, aquamarine salt water, the entry into another world lit with filtered light, feeling like one of the fish that swarmed unafraid in schools around me as I glided effortlessly above the corals and kelps and anemones on the ocean floor.

I realized that fish swim with the same kind of fluidity as birds fly. And I wanted to take that further step—to break through the skin of the sea and lift up, up into the sun's eye, to soar on the updrafts, to view from the height

the flour-white sands hemming the land, the palms and casuarinas like green fringes around the rug of island, the water the color of a gemstone.

Such physical freedom, of fish, of birds, of snorkelers or hang gliders, reminds us of the deeper, more eternal freedoms that entice us toward heaven. What is your heart-dream of heaven? One of the things I long for is release not only from the body but from the earthy bondages of fear and guilt and fatigue and failure that chain both body and mind. I want metamorphosis. Like a pupa developing into a larva and then a flying insect, I yearn to grow toward heaven where my body shell will drop away like the empty skin of a dragonfly.

1 CORINTHIANS 15:51–52;
1 THESSALONIANS 4:17;
2 CORINTHIANS 3:17, author's paraphrase

We will all be changed, in a flash, in the blink of an eye, caught up together in the clouds, to meet the Lord in the air, where the spirit of the Lord is, there is freedom

When my youngest daughter, Kristin, was a small child, I would take her with me wherever I went, as mothers of young children are likely to do. One day, driving to the grocery store in early spring, we passed a field in which a pool of melted snow water glinted under the sun.

Kris was an observant little girl. A light breeze began to ruffle the water's surface and seeing the sun's reflected image broken into shining fragments she cried out, "Look, Mummy, the sun's not round any more!"

At the next stoplight I scribbled the following lines on the back of my grocery list:

SPRING POND

Look how the sun
lies on the low water!

Spread ripple shaped he
has lost roundness:

Light joined to the pond
in fluid fusion

And I, earthy,
wed now to the high sun

Give God a new shape
to shine in.

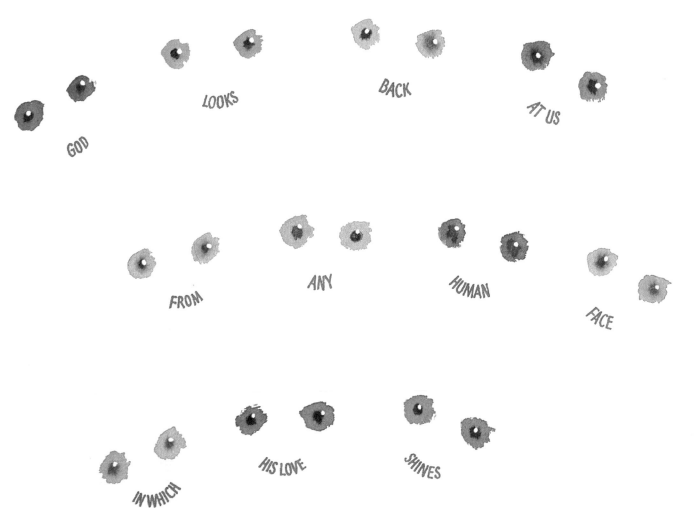

GOD LOOKS BACK AT US FROM ANY HUMAN FACE IN WHICH HIS LOVE SHINES

L.S.

**CITY
SET
ON A
HILL**

*The four wide bowls of oil
cap their square of columns
in the darkened house of God.
The discarded
linen clothes of the priests
have been torn, pulled into wicks,
thousands of them, floating
like stalks in each
bowl, drawing up
the oil of olives
into flowerbeds of light
so that through all Jerusalem
faces glimmer in
the flamelights.*

*At midnight they show us
how to be wicks to bloom
the oil to light;
then, as lumens fill the early bowl
of sky, we learn to become
what we face, showing what
the moon is to the sun—
mirror, solar cell, chloroplast,
soaking up the bright resin
until our own faces
shine like noon.*

We who with unveiled faces all reflect The Lord's Glory are being transformed into his likeness

2 CORINTHIANS 3:18 NIV

The strong imagery of darkness and light pervades the biblical text. Again and again we see the dark night representing ignorance, evil, calamity, death, and damnation, characteristics of a kingdom over which Satan rules. In contrast, light stands for spiritual illumination, clarity, purity, life, all of which thrive in God's domain.

Jesus gave his friends the picture of a city on a hill that "cannot be hidden." Why not? Because a city is full of dwellings where people try to prolong the day with lanterns, oil lamps, candles, or (today) with electric light. Such light is almost impossible to contain. It glints through cracks and crevices, from behind closed doors. And the darker the night, the more brilliantly the light shows.

But no lantern, no modern searchlight or beacon can hold a candle to the sun! Christians today are more like small signal mirrors that flash messages from the desert by reflecting the solar beams. Perhaps Jesus would have used such an image had he lived today.

ABSOLUTE-LY

*If roads went nowhere
and rain fell dry,
if birds crawled low
and worms flew high,
if faces were flat
and the midday sky
looked always dark
and the sun shone square,
if beauty were costly
and God unfair,
if densest earth
were as thin as air,
if clocks went backwards
and grass grew blue
and lions were happiest
in the zoo
and five were the sum
of two and two
would you be me?
might I be you?*

*How would we think
if all sprouts grew down
and the sea churned pink
and the clouds turned brown
and God's face was fixed
in an awful frown?
I'm thankful, I'm thankful
(are you too?)
that grass is green
and sky is blue
and the sun is round
and fact is true
and we can count on
gravity,
and God is good
and beauty free
and, for the sake of
our sanity,
that you are you
and I am me.*

I wrote this child's poem to enflesh in whimsical verse something philosopher Duns Scotus called *haeccitas*, or "this-ness," our intuition that every individual person or thing has its own unique essence and importance. To make this distinctiveness more striking I tried to imagine things in opposite terms from our usual perceptions of them, making my descriptions so outrageous we'd laugh (we all know that grass doesn't "grow blue" and that lions aren't "happiest in the zoo") and in our laughter we might gain something.

C. S. Lewis embodied some pretty hefty theology in his captivating tales *The Chronicles of Narnia,* but families read them for the pure enjoyment. Jesus wanted us to become as free and happy as small children. Again and again he told truth in stories that may have seemed like mere entertainment (in our modern English translations we miss much of Jesus' ironic humor). Wisdom doesn't have to be dour and stodgy; we profit from the enjoyment of play as much as from hard work.

The beauty of play is that it isn't useful for anything but is pleasing to God who wants us to become like little children

PAUL STEVENS
in *Satisfying Work*

35

RELUCTANT PROPHET

*Both were dwellers
in deep places
(one in the dark
bowels of ships
and great fish
and wounded pride.
The other
in the silvery belly
of the seas).*

*Both heard God saying
"Go!"
but the whale
did as he was told.*

Jonah's circumstances were unique; he was sent as a prophet to a warlike enemy people, a Hebrew running from God and angry at God, a man who was thrown overboard into the sea as unlucky, a drowning man who was swallowed by a whale but survived, "damp but undigested." We all have a fellow feeling with Jonah. Like most of us he was stubbornly set on his own way, and he made Jehovah work hard to change his mind.

For Jonah the most difficult thing in the world was to obey. He based his wilful disobedience on his human logic. "Why should I have to preach to the Ninevites?" he asked. "They don't deserve a chance to repent. They're cruel, corrupt, heartless. They *deserve* God's punishment." And when he was finally cornered in Nineveh and the wicked people he was forced to preach to were actually repenting in sackcloth and ashes, Jonah was furious. They should be punished, not forgiven. He felt so bad about it all he wanted to die.

This lesson of obedience to a higher wisdom than our own, an obedience that some creatures in the universe seem to give naturally (whales, for instance) goes against our grain. Today "self-determination" and "freedom" and "individuality" sound like good words, and they make "obedience" sound restrictive and overly meek.

But obedience is a discipline that brings its own insights and rewards. Could it be that the Lord's demands on Jonah (and on us today) were as much for his own growth and benefit as for the sake of the wicked Ninevites?

We might think that
God wanted simply obedience
to a set of rules,
whereas
He really wants
people
of a particular
sort

C.S. Lewis
in *Mere Christianity*

SECTION TWO

I sing the goodness of the Lord, that filled the earth with food;
He formed the creatures with his Word, and then pronounced them good.
Lord, how thy wonders are displayed, where e'er I turn my eye,
If I survey the ground I tread, or gaze upon the sky.

I was searching for a campsite, exploring the wild woods that sloped down to a mountain river in the Canadian Rockies, when I noticed a single deer poised on the bank. She turned her head toward me and "saw" me with her ears. When I think of someone who listens sensitively for God and hears him, I see in my mind this deer, on the alert for the slightest sound or scent.

Sometimes physical seeing becomes impossible, in a blizzard, say, or in the blank blackness of midnight, or when sailing in the middle of a lake, surrounded by fog. We are forced to use our other senses the way blind people learn to do, deprived as they are of the easy, marvelous mechanism of optical vision.

Maybe that was the reason some of the old monastics deliberately practiced sense deprivation. When the mind is no longer distracted and seduced by sounds and smells and sights outside us, it is freed to listen with an inner ear and view the inner landscape of the soul—the baptized imagination.

BLINDFOLD

When someone
pulls down a blind
shuts out seas
sky shore
other ships
shape
of the sun (though
warm still soaks down
blanket filtered)
floats a milky cataract
over every eye:
invisibles thrive and
foghorns celebrate.

In fact, unblunted,
the overlapped
bass warnings
shaking the drenched air
above soft
incessant water-lap
sounds doubly close

advertising their
unseen omnipresence
as if a new trans-
parency has settled
with fog
into all our ears.

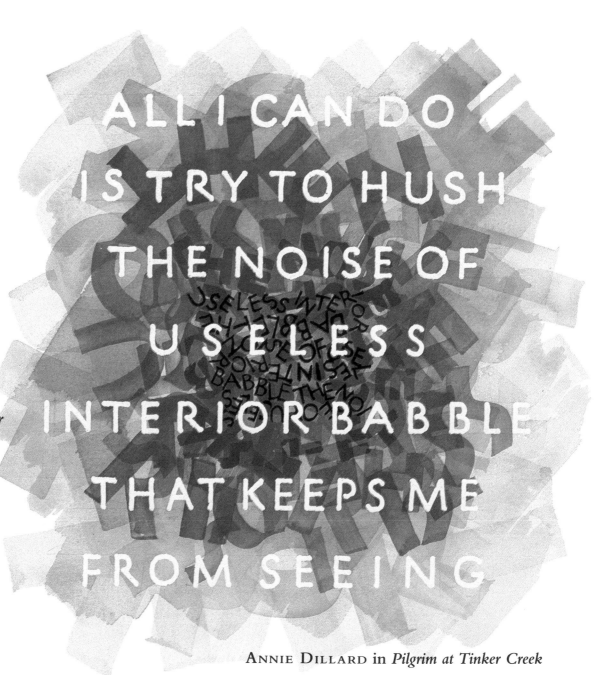

ALL I CAN DO IS TRY TO HUSH THE NOISE OF USELESS INTERIOR BABBLE THAT KEEPS ME FROM SEEING

ANNIE DILLARD in *Pilgrim at Tinker Creek*

41

OF ELMS AND GOD

A glib wind sings.
Wide-blowing branches
are gravid with damp buds
dropping thin brown hulls
like insect wings
into the choked gutters,
and warm airs and showers
are smudging winter's hard-etched edges
fuzzing the dark wood skin
with pale and pendant flowers
until the twigs are diluted to the color of fog.
And now, all my green thoughts
about elms in spring—a tender catalog—
are drawn together, seen
in this one tall and lovely thing
rooted in my door-yard sod.

Yes, it is easy enough
to talk about an elm, but how
do I find words for God?
Spirit is not so readily trapped
in parts of speech,
and to evaporate him to an abstract
is too simple, and not safe.
My verbal reachings for him, like worn and
cast-off clothes, fit him badly. He escapes them
undefined. They are not filled.
He is not found. But if God sent to me
one signal from himself—
if he distilled his deity—
I would be bound
to take his Word for it.

THE TREE AND ME

CHRIST
IS THE
VISIBLE
EXPRESSION
OF THE
INVISIBLE
GOD...
IN HIM
THE FULL
NATURE
OF GOD
CHOSE
TO LIVE

COLOSSIANS 1:15,19 PHILLIPS

When we see an elm tree growing in a square of green grass in front of a house, we can point to it and say, "There's an elm." And we can go on to describe it scientifically, in terms of its botanical species and structure; practically—in terms of the shade it casts or the suitability of its wood for building; poetically—how it looks to us, what emotions it evokes, what it reminds us of, what it seems to mean.

To the tangible, visible, audible objects in the world around us (a bell, a book, a field mouse, a politician, a long-distance runner) we can assign names and values and physical descriptions. They are part of the "known world," which we take for granted because we are so familiar with it.

But how can we know a God who is intangible, invisible, inaudible? To describe him in human terms seems like shrinking him down to our own size, our level of understanding—the One who is infinite, all-powerful, all-knowing.When the only other self-conscious, intelligent, immortal beings we know are people, our tendency is to describe God like a bigger, stronger, better-informed *person.* We have an anthropomorphic view of God.

The only way for us to know what God is really like is *if he describes himself* to us. And at Bethlehem God did that; he shrank *himself* down to the dimensions of a human baby who grew up to become a small-town carpenter; he "got even" with us, as it were, by coming into history at our own level, showing us what God looks like and what his love and sacrifice signify.

Jesus was the Word, God's descriptive message, that still speaks the truth about him. In Christ, God sent the human race an unmistakeable "signal from himself." And we must be daring enough to take his Word for it!

THE OMNIPRESENCE

REMINDERS FLICKER AT US FROM
ODD ANGLES, NOR WILL HE BE IGNORED
WE SIGHT HIM IN UNLIKELY PLACES
OATHS AND DATES AND EMPTY TOMBS
GOD. HIS PRINT IS EVERYWHERE
STAMPED ON THE MACRO AND THE MICROCOSM
FEATHERS, SHELLS, BERRIES, BIRDS' BRIGHT EYES
STARS, CELLS SPEAK HIS DIVERSITY
THE MULTIPLICITY OF LEAF AND LIGHT
SAYS GOD. WIND SENSED
BUT UNSEEN BREATHES THE OLD
METAPHOR AGAIN. SEASONS ARE HIS
SIGNATURE. THE DOUBLE HELIX
SPELLS HIS SPIRAL NAME
FAITH SUMMONS HIM, AND DOUBT
BLOWS ONLY THE SHEEREST SKEIN
OF MIST ACROSS HIS FACE

In the hot noon sun of a summer day I went with two of my daughters, Robin and Kristin, and my grand-daughter Lindsay, to a raspberry farm, with acres of bushes in green rows where you can pick your own berries and save some pennies. There we plucked, for eating and for making jam, twelve pounds of raspberries—huge hybrids, sweet, red-velvet pendants ripe enough to drop into our hands and thence into the plastic buckets slung around our necks.

As we slowly passed between the tall green thickets of bushes, starting and stopping, our fingers stained, our mouths tart with the taste of summer, we would be sure we had thoroughly stripped a certain bush. Then, as we crouched lower, we could see from the new angle all the hidden treasures that remained—berries hanging like red hearts, hiding behind the leaves, waiting for our nimble fingers.

I felt sad for the ones that never got picked (no one took the trouble to go slowly enough or search for them carefully enough), for the ones that seemed too small or too hard to reach. All that slow ripening, as the rains fell and the short, cool days turned long and warm—for nothing—fruit without fruitfulness.

Unpicked raspberries are like the ideas we never discover because we see and think superficially, like the precious people we ignore, like the images of the holy hinted at in creation, like the glimpses of God we miss because our eyes are half-closed or our attention distracted. Harvesting ideas, loving ordinary people, seeing correspondences between the seen and unseen worlds, and gleaning glimpses of God—such tasks, like berry picking, take time, thoroughness, and the willingness to crouch in the sandy soil, to peer upwards, to lift aside the raspberry leaves, to see deep to the heart of each bush—to penetrate its leafy green reality and value what we find there.

How odd that God humbles himself to be seen in the most ordinary, everyday, taken-for-granted stuff of creation! Yet his image is stamped wherever we turn our eyes. The clues to his reality are under our feet, they brush our hands, they rustle in our ears, they mark our bare legs with their sharpness, and they burn our eyes with their color. We are faced so often with things we know but still need to learn. How marvelous it is that realities as mundane as leaves, sunlight, berries, and the delighted cries of young children, are lenses through which we may find God.

If your heart is straight with God,

then every creature will be to you a mirror of life, and a book of holy doctrine.

THOMAS À KEMPIS in *The Imitation of Christ*

CIRCLES

The circle is a universal symbol. As we look around us, we see circles everywhere. The poem suggests only a few of an almost inexhaustible list.

Love is another universal: Our hunger to be loved is our most basic human need; the giving of our love to meet that need is a primal, God-given, human response.

Love and circles seem to be reciprocal; each images and suggests the other.

We arrive at the knowledge of God from other things.

ST. THOMAS AQUINAS

I SING OF CIRCLES, ROUNDED THINGS,
APPLES AND WREATHS AND WEDDING RINGS,
AND DOMES AND SPHERES,
AND FALLING TEARS,
WELL-ROUNDED MEALS,
WATER WHEELS, BOTTOMS OF BELLS
OR WAILING-IN WELLS;

RAIN DROPPING, GOLDEN IN THE AIR
OR SILVER ON YOUR SHINING HAIR;
PEBBLES IN PEWTER-COLORED PONDS
MAKING CIRCLES, ROUNDS ON ROUNDS;
THE CURVE OF A REPEATING RHYME;
THE CIRCLE OF THE FACE OF TIME,
BEYOND THESE CIRCLES I CAN SEE THE CIRCLE OF ETERNITY.

DOES PASSING OF EACH SEASON FAIR
MAKE OF THE FOUR A NOBLE SQUARE?
NO, FOR TO EACH THE OTHERS LEND
A CYCLIC, CURVING, RHYTHMIC BLEND.
REMEMBER, SPRING IN SUMMER GONE
COMES ROUND AGAIN—NEW SPRING COMES ON,

THE CIRCLE IN THE EAGLE'S EYE
MIRRORS THE CIRCLE OF THE SKY;
THE BLUE HORIZON, END TO END,
OVER EARTH'S NEVER-ENDING BEND.
THE ARC OF LOVE FROM GOD TO MEN ORBITING, GOES TO HIM AGAIN.
MY LOVE, TO LOVING GOD ABOVE, CAPTURES ME IN THE ROUND OF LOVE.

Last spring my journal recorded a sudden change: "All the rain, sleet, melting ice, and warming southerly winds mean that there is too much water for the sodden ground to absorb—and there's no place for it to go. Every ditch and furrow and stream brims and glitters with water. As I travel the country roads
I see the sky reflected in places I've never seen it before!

"Each night the temperature dips. Frost catches and controls the flooding until the next day. But during last night's darkness the level of the river dropped dramatically, leaving the saplings along its banks collared with lacy scallops of ice, with the black water churning away two feet below."

Contrasts—warm to cold, high to low, shadow to brightness, smooth to rough—without each we lose the meaning of the other. Without struggle and storm the slick, sunlit days would dream along, serene and unremarkable, taken for granted. Without the dry, hopeless stretches in our emotional or spiritual seasons we might get bored with blessing; grace might seem stale.

Change and renewal dance into our lives dynamically, intersecting the humdrum, with its flatness and decay. I praise my Creator for building into our universe some extraordinary excursions into the unknown, for planning the contrasts and shifts of seasons, for the infinity of space as well as the gentle glow of light shining through a leaf or the wood grain in a floorboard.

INTERPLAY

down
makes
up seem taller
black
sharpens white
flight
firms earth
underfoot
labor
blesses birth
with
later sleep
after silence
each sound
sings
dull clay
shines the
bright coin
in the pot
lemon
honeys its
sweet sequel
and my dark
distress
shows comfort
to be heaven
sent

The dark is as real as the light;

God allows us to experience both

so we will know the difference.

L.S.

HOW TO PAINT A PROMISE IN JANUARY

for Lauren

Here in my winter breakfast room,
the colors of rainbows are
reduced to eight solid lozenges in a
white metal tray. The child's brush
muddies them to gray in a
glass of water. Even the light breaks down
as it pushes through the rain-streaked
windows and polishes the wooden table
imperfectly.

Green leaves always turn
brown. Summer died into the dark days
a long while ago; it is hard even to
remember what it was like, stalled
as I am in this narrow slot of time
and daylight.

Until I look down again
and see, puddling along the paper,
under a painted orange sun
primitive as the first spoked wheel,
the ribbon of colors flowing out of
my granddaughter's memory—a new
rainbow, arc-ing wet over strokes of grass
green enough to be true.

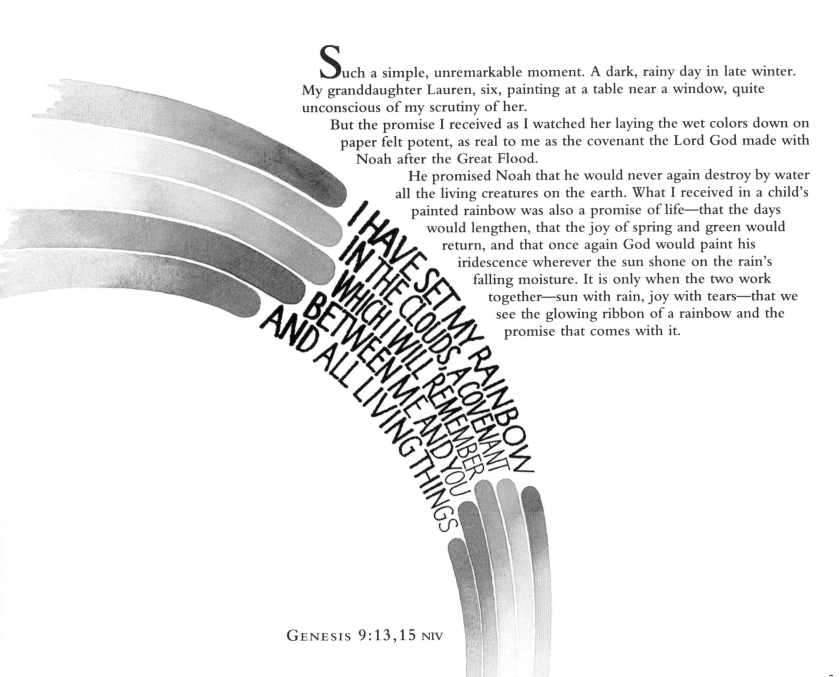

Such a simple, unremarkable moment. A dark, rainy day in late winter. My granddaughter Lauren, six, painting at a table near a window, quite unconscious of my scrutiny of her.

But the promise I received as I watched her laying the wet colors down on paper felt potent, as real to me as the covenant the Lord God made with Noah after the Great Flood.

He promised Noah that he would never again destroy by water all the living creatures on the earth. What I received in a child's painted rainbow was also a promise of life—that the days would lengthen, that the joy of spring and green would return, and that once again God would paint his iridescence wherever the sun shone on the rain's falling moisture. It is only when the two work together—sun with rain, joy with tears—that we see the glowing ribbon of a rainbow and the promise that comes with it.

I HAVE SET MY RAINBOW IN THE CLOUDS, A COVENANT WHICH I WILL REMEMBER BETWEEN ME AND YOU AND ALL LIVING THINGS

GENESIS 9:13,15 NIV

**SOME
CHRISTMAS
STARS**

*The planets blaze behind the hill.
Snow stars glint from the wooden sill.
A spider spins her silver still*

*within your darkened stable shed:
in asterisks her webs are spread
to ornament your manger bed.*

*Where does a spider find the skill
to sew a star? Invisible,
obedient, she works your will*

*with her swift silences of thread.
I weave star-poems in my head;
the spider, wordless, spins instead.*

In our astonishingly loud, verbal world, where achievements are arrogantly proclaimed and every new enterprise is ushered in with a blast and a clatter, it is tranquilizing to see how some small creatures, whose intelligence is mere instinct, who aren't concerned with reputation or credibility, perform their beautiful, ordinary tasks in perfect silence. Yet though spiders, for instance, perform in a kind of private obedience to their calling, they seem to give as much attention to detail and form as if their work were to be exhibited to the whole world.

Another thing. The spider is not easily discouraged. Wipe away her work of art with a clumsy sweep of your elbow and next night she'll do it over for you. This is her vocation—to spin, to weave, to wait, to entangle. She is wholly committed to it; nothing but death will interrupt her persistence.

With my camera as companion, I stalked through the early mist this morning, with the milky light of the sun pressing down, its silver tracing the edges of every wet branch and bud. I noticed how the moisture had condensed along the spider threads in pendant half-circles between the twigs, turning the silk, which I might otherwise have passed without a glance, into star-shaped snares and glistening necklets of crystal.

An asterisk (that twinkling, star-shaped typographical figure whose name springs from the same root as "star") calls attention to something, or footnotes it for our enlightenment. Highlighted for me this morning by moisture of mist is the invisible web of the spider. It tells me to be spider-like, creating in unself-consciousness what I have been called to create— some footnote to the work of my Creator.

Beauty and grace are performed whether or not we sense them

The least we can do is try to be there

ANNIE DILLARD
in *Pilgrim at Tinker Creek*

53

THE AMPHIBIAN

WARM
AFTER A WHILE ON A HOT ROCK,
DRUNK WITH SKY, THE GREEN
SILK OF HER SKIN SHRIVELS
WITH WIND. WITH A WET, SINGULAR
SOUND, THEN, SHE CREASES
THE SILVER FILM, TURNS FLUID,
HER WEBBED TOES ACCOMPLISHING
THE DARK DIVE TO WATER BOTTOM AND
THE LONG SOAK, UNTIL HER LUNGS,
SPUN FOR AIR, URGE HER UP
FOR BREATH. SHE MOVES
IN TWO WORLDS, CAUGHT BETWEEN
UPPER AND UNDER, SHE CAN NEVER
BE HOME, RESTLESS; EITHER
WITHERING FOR WET,
AND THE NETHER OOZE,
OR NOSTRILS ACHING TO FILL
HER BUBBLE LUNGS WITH FREE AIR,
HEART THUMPING, TYMPANUM
THROAT PULSING TO FLOOD
THE DARKENING AIR WITH LOUD
FROG SONG

In my search for metaphors by which to see and shape my life, l spent a year viewing myself in the skin of a green frog. It seemed to me a perfect image for the dilemma of the person linked to God by personal relationship, drawn toward heaven, but of necessity still human, "of the earth, earthy," tied to a physical body with all its needs and impulses.

Most frogs, amphibious, designed to breathe air but swim water, cannot exist for long in either element. Frog (as I named myself) must pivot continually between the upper-air level and the underwater level. In air, she will dehydrate and wither; submerged too long in water, her lungs will be deprived of oxygen and she will drown.

I, too, am restless, shifting up and down, pulled in two directions. I have already breathed the air of heaven, by virtue of the Spirit now resident in me, but I'm not yet ready for heaven, ill-equipped for its fierce air; it is too bright, too sharp, too clean, too intense for my fleshly frailty. Having emerged from the sludge at the bottom of the pond, I am sucked down into it again by my humanity, only to be dragged up again by my need to breathe.

What, on earth, is the job of a frog—her reason for existing? To replicate herself? To keep the insect population in check? To look decorative on a lily pad? To inspire poets? I think she is meant to exhibit the attributes of *frogness* for which she was created.

I ask myself the same question—what am I here for? If I read my own nature and my Bible aright, I am to be a link between earth and heaven, to be in relationship with both persons and the Person. I am to be poised for upward movement, with one foot in heaven, one on earth. And I am to fulfill the true humanity I was created for, which suggests an earthiness discontented with mere earth.

Here we have

no continuing city,

but we look

for one to come.

HEBREWS 13:14

author's paraphrase

55

UNDER THE SNOWING

Under the snowing
the leaves lie still.
Brown animals sleep
through the storm, unknowing,
behind the bank
and the frozen hill.
And just as deep
in the coated stream
the slow fish grope
through their own dark,
stagnant dream.

Who on earth would hope
for a new beginning
when the crusted snow
and the ice start thinning?
Who would ever know
that the night could stir
with warmth and wakening
coming, creeping,
for sodden root and fin and fur
and other things lonely and
cold and sleeping?

HIDDEN THINGS ARE ONLY WAITING

Hibernation is a mysterious process. In certain latitudes the cycle of seasons comes around inevitably to winter, and as if to protect themselves, waiting
it out in safe, dark seclusion, many animals enter a different state. Their breathing and heart rates become almost imperceptible, body temperatures lower, and metabolism slows. Sleep takes over. It is like a quiet, temporary death.

In the summer that follows, the animals—bears, other furred mammals and fish—have been restored to full vitality, consuming quantities of food, actively foraging, hunting, mating, reproducing. What has happened in the interim?

Spring, the renewal of warmth and light, makes all the difference.

And it is so in the realms of the soul and the spirit. We, along with the rest of the created universe, await the ultimate spring of heaven and restoration to our full faculties. Light will spring up and flood us with life, redeeming ("buying back") the long, dark night
of waiting.

All creation has been groaning...
creation waits in eager expectation...
creation itself will be liberated
from bondage to decay, and brought into glorious freedom

ROMANS 8:22,19,21 NIV

57

**WINTER CHESTNUT:
FIVE HAIKU**

*Behind me—a thud
on the sidewalk, padded with
leaves like open hands.*

*I turn. It is like
a key. The jade womb unlocks,
birthing you at my feet.*

*New as a baby
you hold the heavy secrets
of growing, dying.*

*Now fingered and shrunk,
your Fall gloss faded, you look
as spent as I feel,*

*But you still ride my
raincoat pocket—Christ's coal for
my five cold fingers.*

It was late autumn in Vancouver, a hiatus of chilling rain—the year too far gone for warmth and golden days, too early for Christmas.

I left a friend's house after a very early-morning Great Books discussion group, descended the wooden steps, and moved along the walk toward my car. Under my feet the concrete sidewalk felt mushy. Looking down, I realized that it was so thickly carpeted with wide, yellow chestnut leaves that the pavement was completely covered. The parent chestnut tree loomed above me, muddy gold in the early gray of the rain-filled dawn. A long day of reading, tutorials, and teaching lay before me. I was already tired. It was cold. I shivered.

Then, I felt as much as heard a faint plop behind me. As I turned and looked back, the green, spiny husk of the chestnut that had just thudded on the leaves split open, and the glossy, brown nucellus rolled toward me, as if heaven had not only dropped me a gift but had unwrapped it to save me the trouble.

I love chestnuts, the silk feel of them, their pregnant weight, their uneven roundness, their satin shine. This one seemed to gleam with potential life at a time of year when everything else was dying or rotting or going to sleep. I picked up the small present and put it in my raincoat pocket. My day had been renewed.

In time my chestnut lost some of its plump gloss, but it stayed in my pocket all winter. Every time I fingered it I was warmed by the thought of its Giver and the timing of the gift.

THE ONLY IMPERATIVE THAT NATURE UTTERS IS LOOK LISTEN ATTEND

CS Lewis in The Four Loves

DESIGNER

How elegant the egg—
though breakable, benign
and self-complete!
Its formal shape how fine—
sans superfluity
and with what firm
economy of line.
How easily it fits
the palm,
catches and holds
a shine,
enters the eye,
and rests its case
for the divine—
for elemental,
unimproveable design!

Ovals and circles—any spherical or elliptical shapes—fascinate me. I find a perfection, a completeness to smooth stones and green peas and lima beans. I love eggs in particular, their thin, fragile shells smooth as skin, neatly packaging primal bird life. White hens' eggs or brown, the gentle color of eucalyptus bark, look as pure and feel as clean as silk.

They remind me of the way my mother-in-law used to break an egg on the edge of a bowl—the sharp sound of it, the splash of yolk and white—when she baked bread. She mixed her bread dough several times a week adding to the eggs, flour, and yeast whatever leftovers caught her fancy in the icebox that day—cold oatmeal porridge, mashed potatoes, cottage cheese, or the baby's applesauce. Each time the bread came from the oven uniquely delicious, fragrant, and wholesome.

I want my writing and my life to be like that. Whether we are poets, or parents, or teachers, or artists, or gardeners, we must start where we are and use what we have. In the process of creation and relationship, what seems mundane and trivial may show itself to be holy, precious, part of a pattern.

LISTEN TO YOUR Life TOUCH · TASTE · SMELL your way to the holy, hidden heart of it because ALL MOMENTS ARE KEY MOMENTS

and life itself is grace

FREDERICK BUECHNER from *Now & Then*

61

INTO ORBIT
for Doug Engle

Eyes wise behind their rims,
shoelaces flying, our eight-year-old visitor
has escaped the house. We tell him the swing
was put up wrong—the ropes not allowed to hang
loose before we knotted them to the high branch,
so that the two descenders twist always to a
triangle, its bottom held open by the wooden slat.
He unwinds it, seats himself, and pumps into a wide
ellipse that veers, throws him off balance
against the trunk. Curious still in spite
of bruises, he leaps down, counter-spins
the darn thing, and spread-eagles on the grass
underneath, watching upward as it careens and stops
and ties itself again into a spiral
tight as DNA, tenacious as original sin.

In the swing's circling, can he see the turn,
the inward pull of self's dark gravity, the need
to push free, fly the wind, fling out beyond
release, find his own trajectory
in an expanding universe?

The small, red-headed boy, the son of old friends, was bored with our adult conversation. Through the window he saw the old swing suspended from one of our oaks. We had hung it for our own kids long before, but it had always twisted itself into a single strand rather than hanging double, straight and free. Insatiably curious and intelligent as the children of older parents often are, Doug had to find out why.

Watching his investigation from the house, I was struck with the correspondence between the twisted swing and the inward pull—the knotting of the self. Just as Doug had to untwirl the swing, he would have to discover how to be free, through grace, from his tight-knit human bondage to self and self-consciousness.

We are powerless in ourselves to do this. We must each fly the wind of the Spirit to find our own new trajectory in God's great, expanding universe of the heart and soul.

WE MUST EACH
FLY THE WIND OF THE SPIRIT
TO FIND OUR OWN TRAJECTORY
IN GOD'S GREAT
EXPANDING UNIVERSE
OF THE HEART AND SOUL

Wherever the spirit of the Lord is our souls are set free.

2 CORINTHIANS 3:17 PHILLIPS

Letters are often lifelines. During his terminal illness, my husband and I needed the links of phone calls and letters to feel our connections with friends who loved us and prayed for us.

A note from my friend Maxine Hancock described for us how she and her husband, out walking their prairie farm in the darkening evening, had heard the strong pulse of a flock of ducks flying overhead.

The sound of the wing-beat of ducks is a quickening symbol of moving power. In her words we could almost hear the sound, feel the brush of air on our cheeks. She had translated it for us into an image of the Holy Spirit's arrival at Pentecost and brought the sense of his comforting vitality into our lives when we were feeling weak and disheartened.

May God the Father bless you,

God the Son heal you,

and God the Holy Spirt

give you strength.

Benediction from *The Book of Common Prayer*

She said she heard the sound
for the first time
that evening.

THE COMFORTING

They were walking the back pasture
to river edge
not talking, taking in
the half-moon, breathing the
lucid silence, when at their left
a wind seemed to lift and he said
"listen" and "there they are."

And she saw that the wind-sound
was wing-sound,

that

a cloud of ducks
was moving the sky, without
a cry the pulse of two hundred
feathered wings
shook the whole night
She knew then
how the Comforter had sounded ...
the strong breath of his arrival,
the Spirit wing-beat
filling their ears

And knowing our need of comfort
in a dark, chill night,
she folded the sound into words
in a little card
and sent it to us with her love.

SECTION THREE

There's not a plant or flower below, but makes thy glories known;
And clouds arise, and tempests blow, by order from thy throne;
While all that borrows life from thee is ever in thy care,
And everywhere that I can be, God's love is present there.

SPRING

THE AIR IS FILLED WITH SOUTH...
BREATH WHICH THOUGH SOFT, UNSEEN
PANTS WARM FROM SOME FAR TROPIC MOUTH
AND MISTS THE WORLD WITH GREEN.

Afriend once told me, "Spring has three stages: the spring of light, the spring of running water, the spring of green."

Light is a word with double meaning. The first harbinger of spring, light literally *lightens* us, easing from us the weight of winter. Each noon the sun arcs higher, and the nights shrink at their edges as the days stretch out, taking over, gathering the minutes into hours at each end; the light lengthens and strengthens, and thus spring lifts and lightens our spirits. Because we are newly lit it seems as if this hopeful "lightness" penetrates our bones and translates itself into a buoyancy that is physical, as if gravity has lost some of its power and we can *spring*—leaping about with enthusiasm and cheerful ease, like people on the moon. On my walk this morning I had a spring in my step, (in more than one sense). The grass glittered in the melting frost. The air was intoxicatingly fresh, mild, and exhilarating.

The spring of *running water*—I have walked through that, too, when my eyes and bereaved heart overflowed with tears that matched the weeping from the skies. But combined with the growing warmth that comes with light, the running water ushers in the third spring—the vernal equinox—the spring of *green.*

As I walk today, the sun beams at me from high in the eastern sky, writing its warm promise first on my back and then, as I turn homeward, on my face. I finish my accustomed circuit with the curlicue into Wayne Oaks Lane and my own driveway. Along the way the edges of the turf, the sun-warmed banks and sheltered spots, are tinged on the sunny slopes with verdure—spears of grass pushing up through the pale straw that was last summer's sod. Daffodil leaves spike along the hedges. Because of the increasing hours of light and the abundant rain, the spring of green has begun!

I am greening too. The winter of darkness and grief that froze me after my husband's death is melting away. I am beginning to lift my face to the sun again. There are traces of fresh growth in me, of "beauty instead of ashes." This morning I read verdant words from the Song of Solomon, and I know experientially what they mean. "My lover spoke and said to me, 'Arise, my darling, my beautiful one, and come with me. See! The winter is past; the rains are over and gone. Flowers appear on the earth; the season of singing has come'" Song of Solomon 2:10-11 [NIV].

How fresh, O Lord,

how sweet and clean

Are thy returns!

Ev'n as the flowers in spring;...

Grief melts away

Like snow in May

As if there were

no such cold thing.

"The Flower" by George Herbert

LET HIM HEAR

ALL LESS
THAN MAPLE LEAVES
OUR EARS ARE BLUNT OUR EARS ARE THICKER
HOT-BLOODED, WE LISTEN HOW CAN WE HEAR HIM BLESS
FOR NO CALL THE BRANCHES WITH
BUT THIS IS THE DAY HIS SECRET WORD-DOWN FALL
THE TREES OBEY SO THAT THE STILL AIR
GOD & THE SEASON DANCES? WE CONFESS
LINE THE WOOD, WALL ALL WE CAN DO
TO WALL, WITH GOLD IS COCK OUR HEADS
LEAF, FACET THE VIEW TO CATCH THE LEAVES' THIN
FLECK THE SUN'S EYE WHISPERED ANSWER:
WITH MOTES THAT YES & YES & YES
FALL & FALL & FALL

T H E   L E A V E S   H A V E   E A R S

Have you ever walked in the woods on a windless autumn day when, as if by inaudible command, a scatter of golden leaves let go above you and begin to float down from their parent branches, whispering their obedience, their "yes" to God, as they land on the forest floor and gild it seamlessly with "gold leaf"?

The trees in the forest listen to their Creator. With every season he whispers his old/new words; they hear him attentively and obey him instantly. But we humans are different; a separate created order infinitely more complex and clever, we have been given some risky gifts—self-consciousness, reflective intelligence, imagination, and a free will that makes wide-reaching choices and decisions. Yet in spite of these advantages we have been rendered tone-deaf by sin, and although we ought gratefully to return our gifts to God, we choose often to serve our own petty purposes and ignore his voice.

Unlike the trees, people aren't rooted in one place; we are constantly pulled off course by life's distractions. The small, interior voice of God is drowned out in human hubbub. When I read Jesus' urgent plea for followers who have "ears to hear," I feel his longing for listening ears. He wants his Word to be made flesh again in each one of us.

Lord, even as we're thinking about this process and how it should happen, can we hear your voice with our inner ears? Yes. And as we walk among the trees and realize suddenly why autumn is called Fall, (the leaves in the still air begin to float down as if by your secret command), we know you are telling us about our own need to listen and obey. Our inner ears are open toward you. Widen and fill them with your messages.

Hear him, ye deaf,

this praise, ye dumb

your loosened tongues

employ!

"O For a Thousand Tongues to Sing"

by CHARLES WESLEY

OMNIPOTENCE

He asks of us a big faith—the moving
of mountains. It fits—
he was the one who once made a Big Bang,
spins a galaxy like a child's top,
cradles our world—a marble in his palm.
But can he pop a jammed hood or deflate
an aneurism? Is he deft enough to splint
a broken finger, split an apple
between us, or flick
a loose lash from my eye?

He's big, all right—his face
could brood from Mount Rushmore.
But I ache for someone my size to bring me
hot chocolate, brush my hair, slip
between my sheets, read to me in bed.
For a lover like that I'd move a mountain
one stone at a time.

It's the ache of being alone. All of us feel it sooner or later. For the unmarried it's now, every day, every night. For couples, it's an inevitable and unwelcome prospect; unless separation comes through instantaneous death for both at once, they must anticipate that splitting of the "one flesh" in which one partner exits, moving away from the other in space and time. The seam of marriage is unraveled by death or, even more unhappily, divorce.

After the numbing paralysis of bereavement I tried all the ploys recommended to widows—"develop new interests," "keep busy," "reach out to others in need," "give yourself time," "pamper yourself," "just rest in the Lord." But the emptiness, the aloneness refused easy answers; it had to be
lived through.

But it was during that time that I felt, more than in any other crisis time in my life, the need to know experientially that my God is personal. It wasn't hard for me to recognize the power of God in creation, to see the evidences of his handiwork in nature—the seasons, the earth textures, the colors of flowers and plumage and sunsets, the three-dimensional flow of earth-life before me, like a living mural. But I wanted a God "with skin."

And then I held in my arms my first grandson. And the squirm and squall of the baby reminded me that I did, indeed, have a God "with skin." In Mary's womb God had formed himself into a baby much like little Jack, who sucked and slept and grew muscles and got tired and loved his friends.

l am a friend of Jesus. I *have* a God with skin and a lover who stays with me night and day; my faith in him and his closeness may move the mountain of loneliness.

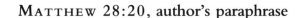

LOOK I AM always with you

MATTHEW 28:20, author's paraphrase

My friend Martha was on the phone, her voice barely controlling her panic.

"Please pray," she said, "I've lost my rings." She had been spring cleaning and had removed her wedding and engagement rings for safekeeping. When the job was done, she looked for her rings. Like many married women, she felt rather naked without them.

But the rings were gone. Worse, she couldn't recall where she had put them for "safety." She and her husband searched the now-glistening kitchen—shelves, cupboards, drawers, hooks, nooks, probing even the drain of the kitchen sink. Nothing. The precious twin symbols of their marriage had disappeared without trace.

"But they couldn't have just *vanished*," I protested over the phone line. "Diamonds and gold don't simply evaporate. They're there, somewhere."

The incident traveled around and around in my mind. I began to ponder the persistence of material things, and beyond physical realities I thought of all the other precious gifts that we give, and are given, and of the words we speak into the air. Even though they are invisible, nothing will ever obliterate them. I thought of the lavishing of love on someone dear who may, at the time, appear to be indifferent to it, so that the love seems wasted.

Over the following years I sometimes asked Martha if the rings had ever turned up. Always the answer was, "No. Not yet." And so I wrote a poem, which is one way I have of working through a puzzle.

BUT NOT FORGOTTEN

Whether or not
I find the missing thing
it will always be
more than my thought of it.
Silver-heavy, somewhere it winks
in its own small privacy
playing
the waiting game with me.

And the real treasures
do not vanish.

The precious loses no value
in the spending.
A piece of hope spins out
bright, along the dark,
and is not lost in space;
verity is a burning boomerang;
love is out orbiting and will
come home.

Rejoice with me

for that which was lost

has been found!

LUKE 15:9, author's paraphrase

Eight years later, Martha and her husband decided to renovate their kitchen. As they lowered one of the old metal cabinets from the wall, they could hear a muffled rattle. For the first time they realized that the shelf was hollow, with slits at each end, and they began to wonder and then to hope. They turned the shelf upside down and shook it. A hairpin appeared, then a couple of paper clips, and then—then the rings fell, gleaming one by one, into Martha's hands—gifts twice-given.

When she called me, with elation and excitement in her voice, she reminded me of the New Testament woman who lost one of her betrothal coins and who, when she found it, celebrated with her friends and neighbors. And I was deeply glad, not only because Martha had found her precious rings, but because my poem had proven to be true.

75

A SONG FOR SIMPLICITY

There are some things that should be as they are:
plain, unadorned, common, and all-complete;
things not in a clutter, not in a clump,
unmuddled and unmeddled with;
the straight, the smooth, the salt, the sour, the sweet.
For all that's timeless, untutored, untailored, and untooled;
for innocence unschooled;
for unplowed prairies, primal snow and sod,
water unmuddied, wind unruled,
for these, thank God....

I am fifty miles into Iowa, driving to a speaking engagement. Here and there the flat prairie landscape is enlivened by spring plowing. Between long, uncultivated stretches I see disking machines, like ships plowing the waves of the fields, trailing clouds of dust thick as sea-mist and wakes of turf folded back, rounded and shining as waves, but solid. Small clumps of trees lie like islands around which the bare ocean of landscape stretches, cut in sharp relief against the simple immensity of the sky. Now and then a single tree breaks the flatness of a plowed field.

This has been a day of solitude on almost deserted highways with no towns for twenty or thirty miles at a stretch. Only the plows and a now-and-then barn glimpsed on the horizon give me a clue that this land is inhabited. The earth is bare and dun-colored. The cool weather of this past week has put spring on hold until today, and the south sides of banks and ditches are still mottled with rags of snow. The tree islands are innocent of leaves, though I can see the fattening buds. Their fringed tops let light through, and their nakedness makes for a clarity, a straightforwardness, a disclosure that the lush growth of summer obscures.

Later, in the home of my hosts I voice a question: "Why do farmers sometimes leave one lone tree standing in the middle of a field?" I get an eminently practical answer from the man who grew up on a farm: "So that when they're plowing, they have something to rest the eye on. It helps them keep the furrows straight."

So. Since then, whenever I drive the prairie, I look for the lone trees—the plowman's navigational buoys set in seas of soil. I ask myself, can I be for someone else an interruption in the horizon, a landmark, a directional signal, a simplicity on which they can rest the eye and know they're going straight?

Matthew 6:22
author's paraphrase

HIGHWAY SONG FOR FEBRUARY 14
"Nancy I love you—Danny"—roadside graffito

On overhead and underpass,
beside the road, beyond the grass,

in aerosol or paint or chalk
the stones cry out, the billboards talk.

On rock and wall and bridge and tree,
boldly inscribed for all to see,

hearts and initials intertwine
their passionate, short-lived valentine.

I'm listening for a long Lover
whose declaration lasts forever:

from field and flower, through wind and breath,
in straw and star, by birth and death,

his urgent language of desire
flickers in dew and frost and fire.

This earliest spring that I have seen
hints at his tender love—in green,

and on my windshield, clear and plain,
my Dearest signs his name in rain.

Humans can't seem to leave the landscape alone, untouched, unmeddled with. What causes us to carve our names or initials on our school desks or on park benches or tree trunks? What impels us to spray paint them on wayside rocks and bridges? We want our identity to be remembered, our love immortalized. We want to leave a message to the next generation: "I was here. Don't forget me!" or "Remember. We two were so much in love." There are other, less blatant messages to be read, if we open our eyes to decode the clues. Our heavenly Lover's devotion and passion for us are evident in the life of the earth around us, in every natural phenomenon—rounded beach stones, sprouting wheat along the furrows, water running clear over rocks, the spiral shape of a shell, the uncorrupted sky. Everything can speak of God, if we take time to look and listen, to see with the eyes of the heart, which he has promised to enlighten. Can we read his letters to us? "Listen to me. I cherish you. Once I came to live among you so that you could know my love. Now, here in the rain on your windshield, the frost on the stubble, the warm breath of the breeze, is another love note. Read it, and hold it in your heart."

Anything can make us look;

only love can make us see.

ARCHIBALD MACLEISH

**BUT THE
WORD OF GOD
WILL STAND
FOREVER**
Isaiah 40:6–8

*All flesh is grass
and I can feel myself growing
an inch an hour in the dark,
ornamented with a lyric dew
fine as glass beads, my edges
thin as green hair.*

*All flesh—
and there are seventeen kinds
of us in this one corner of the
hayfield, along with clover,
oxalis, chicory, Wild Wilber—
close enough cousins for a
succulent hay.*

*Early mornings
we all smell of rain
enough to drown the microscopic
hoppers and lubricate snails
along their glistening paths:
a fine, wet fragrance, but not
so sweet as this evening, after
the noon scythe.*

*No longer,
now, are the windows of air
hung with our lace, embroidered
with bees. Laid low, we raise
a new incense, and under the brief
stubble, our roots grieve.*

THE GOD WHO MIXES HIS METAPHORS

In summer I mow my lawn every week, unconscious of anything but satisfaction as the green velvet unrolls in ribbons behind me. Sometimes, though, as I smell the sweet spice of the cut grass, I hear God's word through his prophet, Isaiah, telling me that *I am grass.* As I sniff my way into grass's greenness, its dew-bathed moisture in the early light, I also learn what it means to be as vulnerable as grass is to the scythe or the mower.

Isaiah says: "All people are grass, their constancy is like the flower of the field.... The grass withers, the flower fades; but the word of our God will stand forever." The greenest blades of grass will turn brown in a drying wind or be severed in an instant by a sharp blade and laid in swathes on the stubble to dry. And I bear the same stamp of frailty, weakness, mortality.

So it is a real surprise to read elsewhere in Isaiah's prophecy, (Isaiah 61:3) that as one of the people of God I am proclaimed an "oak of righteousness, a planting of the Lord." What could show a greater contrast—slender, perishable grass, growing at the foot of a long-lived, stalwart oak tree whose wood is renowned for its toughness? How could the Lord speak of the same person with two such opposite images?

To understand such seeming contradictions, we must learn to think metaphorically—and sometimes it seems that God mixes his metaphors, when he gives us two opposing statements that are both true. It is paradoxical for me to think of my husband, who died of cancer, in terms of the strength and durability of an oak tree (though in his life of service for God he was truly "a planting of the Lord") and yet affirm that in his death he partook of grass's tenderness and transience and vulnerability. Yet both are true.

LiViNg WiTh CoNtRaDiCtIoNs PrEsEnTs Us NoT wItH a ClOsEd SyStEm BuT wItH a SeRiEs Of OpEn DoOrS

ESTHER DE WAAL in *Living with Contradiction*

EPIGNOSIS

I think to myself the name
of the bird on the front lawn—
robin—wondering
how I can hear so well in my head
the name he doesn't know himself.
Nor does he have a word for sod
or worm or tree or light
yet without names he knows each one
better than I for what it is:
sod
for its solidity and spring
under the trident feet,
the smell of the green tangle,
the clues to the cocked ear
of a thousand roots spreading, or moles
in their blind undertunneling;
worm
for the long, thrilling, elastic pull
from the earth after rain, the wriggle,
the luscious roundness in the throat;
tree
for the swell of buds as the sap hums
up its height, the launching of its
highest branches onto the planes of air;
light
for its slow warmth, its lift and beckon
into the sun's eye, where words
evaporate, and no names are needed.

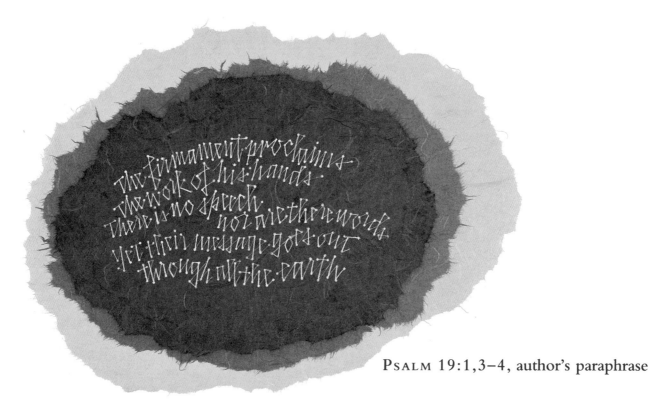

the firmament proclaims
the work of his hands
there is no speech
nor are there words
yet their message goes out
through all the earth

PSALM 19:1,3–4, author's paraphrase

I like to get in touch with the texture of the day as it starts. This works best when I am outside, walking or just sitting very still on my front steps. It is a perception that begins with a detailed observation of the weather—a red sunrise, fog drifting through the oaks, a mackerel sky, or a sky so innocently blue it seems like a God-given present that I have just unwrapped. I am alert for clouds heavy with rain, the angle and force of the breeze, birdsongs, the temperature, and the touch of the air—frosty and sharp or silky and mild.

But I also sense the day's significance by a kind of intuition that comes through listening, thinking how I would describe most accurately what I see, what is going on. That's when I hear the beginning lines of a new poem or think through an unfinished thought that has been biding its time for me until the missing phrases, or links of logic, present themselves in my mind and everything falls into place.

I used to expect God to "answer my prayers" from outside of me, waiting for him to change my circumstances, to alter the equation of my life from some hidden omnipotence beyond me. I am learning now that my very own thoughts, my ideas as a child of God, are often the mind of Christ speaking to me from inside, reminding me in the gentlest, most unsensational way of what I know already but need to learn over again. This is not a knowledge from outside me but integrated with my very person. It has been called epignosis (the Greek word means "superknowledge"—understanding beyond the rational).

But it is hard to hear that inner voice unless I allow myself time and quiet to center down, to focus in. I can find silence indoors, but it seems static. Breathing in the dynamic stillness as the whole creation pauses before God, the psalmist also sensed that "The heavens declare the glory of God...."

83

Although I sometimes knock on my neighbor's kitchen window and we walk together, I also like the aloneness of walking with the countryside as my companion. I never feel really alone because the dogs who "own" each property I pass recognize me instantly, and I them.

Each one enters into a sort of canine hortatory monologue directed at me. It's both a greeting and a warning: "Hello! Yes, I see you and I know you. Don't slow down and be sure to keep your distance. No, not an inch closer, not on your life! I've got my eye on you, and you look trustworthy, but one never knows. Nice day, isn't it? But there'll be rain by evening, just you wait and see. Well, see you tomorrow. Over to you, Clover." And Clover, a German shepherd, or Agamemnon, a black Labrador, starts up a similarly repetitive, companionable, even reassuring series of yips.

The natural rhythms of walking and breathing (inhale for two steps, exhale for three) trigger the rhythms of words and phrases in my mind. Ideas come with the words, and prayers. But it is when the world is very silent—with no bark of dog or breath of wind—that God feeds me with his deeper thoughts. That's when he shows me "the big picture"—puts all the lovely detail of petal and colored leaf and moss and grass into perspective, and I know he arranged it all—for me! I know that my entering into each element of it with delight— the dew-beaded spider web, the waning moon hung low on the western sky like a baroque pearl while the sun breasts the horizon in the east (that tranquil time that is both dusk and dawn), the smell of dew on grass and the color of it, with a point of light at the heart of each silver-green drop—all give God's delight its finishing touch, for didn't he create this place so that he and I could enjoy it together? And we do, Lord.

Loneliness is poverty of self;

solitude is sufficiency without and within.

L.S.

MAY 20: VERY EARLY MORNING

all the field praises him, all
dandelions are his glory, gold
and silver, all trilliums unfold
white flames above their trinities
of leaves, all wild strawberries
and massed wood violets reflect his skies'
clean blue and white,
all brambles, all oxeyes,
all stalks and stems lift to his light,
all young windflower bells
tremble on hair springs for
his carillon touch,
last year's yarrow (raising

brittle star skeletons) tells
age is not past praising,
all small, low, unknown,
unnamed weeds show his impossible greens,
all grasses sing,
tone on clear tone,
all mosses spread a spring-
soft velvet for his feet
and by all means
all leaves, buds, all flowers cup
jewels of fire and ice
holding up
to his kind morning heat
a silver sacrifice.

Now make of our hearts a field to raise your praise

FORECAST

planting
seeds
INEVITABLY
changes
my feelings
A B O U T
rain
rain
rain

One of the inescapable rites of spring is the planting of seeds. Every year, because I find bare patches in my lawn where there is too much shade or not enough rain, I seem destined to scatter new grass seed. And it is a perfectly marvelous feeling, once the seed has been spread and raked into the soil, to hear a gentle rain falling all night, soaking the seed, encouraging it to swell and sprout. Somehow rain, which we often consider a nuisance or a dreary necessity, rounds out the emotional spectrum; its steady falling has the sound of a blessing, once the seed is in.

Why is it that the wild verdure seems to spring up spontaneously without any human help? God must be a great Gardener! As the weather warms, along the verges of all the roads appears the lush green fur of grasses, with seed heads like feathers or lace. Every week new kinds of grass spring up delicately, and earlier varieties darken and thicken. Just observing the shoulders of the road keeps my senses surprised all summer.

In August the wildflower heads form bands of color like hemlines to the roads on either side of me as I walk or drive. In the hard, gravelly edges springs the innocent blue of chicory—fresh and fully open early in the day, withered by noon. Close behind them are the daisy-like Indian paintbrushes in rust and yellow and the black eyes of Susans peering from their brilliant orange faces. Next shine the ribbons of clover, purple and pink and white, decorated with bees. And behind them all, like a white crocheted skirt laid over the fields, is the Queen Anne's lace—a favorite flower in our household; my daughter Robin used an armful of it for her wedding bouquet.

They all combine to make a spectrum of color, painting in my mind a portrait of summer. The Impressionists couldn't have done it better.

I saw another spectrum last July in the foothills of the Cascade Mountains. A double rainbow arched from north to south against a charcoal sky, the inner half-circle spectacularly brilliant, the outer bow, with its colors reversed, paler and more diffused. I couldn't get it all into one exposure on my film. One never can. The camera remembers precisely, but it also frames—pulling rectangles out of the air, fragmenting the whole landscape, focusing on the part rather than the whole. Like poetry. Like most human experience.

I want to see the complete spectrum of life color. I want it to blaze in my imagination, not pale or partial, but bright from the hand of the Creator.

We are here to abet creation

and to witness it,

to notice each thing

so each thing gets noticed...

so that Creation need not play

to an empty house.

ANNIE DILLARD

on *"The Meaning of Life"*

QUILTMAKER

"I make them warm to keep my family from freezing.
I make them beautiful
to keep my heart from breaking."
—prairie woman, 1870

To keep a husband and five children warm,
she quilts them covers thick as drifts against
the door. Through every fleshy square white threads
needle their almost invisible tracks; her hours
count each small suture that holds in place
the raw-cut, uncolored edges of her life.

She pieces each one beautiful and summer bright
to thaw her frozen soul. Under her fingers
the scraps grow to green birds and purple,
improbable leaves; deeper than calico, her mid-winter
mind bursts into flowers. She watches them unfold
between the double stars, the wedding rings.

When the world was created, it would have been enough to have it work, wouldn't it? A functioning universe would have seemed sufficient. To include beauty seems gratuitous, a gift of pure grace. The creation of beauty links us with our Creator. God, the first Quilter of prairies, the prime Painter (sunsets, night skies, forget-me-nots, thunderheads), the archetypal metal Sculptor (mountain ranges), the Composer who heard the whales' strange, sonorous songs in his head long before there were whales to sing them, the Playwright who plotted the sweeping drama of life, the Poet whose Word said it all—

God made us humans in his image; we participate in creative intelligence, giftedness, originality.

Most of all we have the faculty of imagination deep within us, waiting like a seed to be watered and fertilized. Imagination gives us pictures by which to see things the way they *can* be or the way they *are* underneath. The prairie woman, hemmed in with her small children by months of cold and snow, used her imagination redemptively. Around the traditional quilt patterns—double stars, wedding rings—her imagination pieced in the exuberant flowers and leaves that redeemed the long winter, that thawed her soul. She created beauty and richness from the ordinary stuff of life.

Beauty IS TO THE SPIRIT what food is to the flesh It fills an emptiness in you that nothing else under the sun can

FREDERICK BUECHNER in *Whistling in the Dark*

PNEUMA

The wind breathes where it wishes

flows where it flows

THE EYE OF YOUR STORM

SEES FROM THE WILD HEIGHT

Your air augments the world

tearing away dead wood

TESTING, TOUGHENING ALL TREES

spreading all seeds

THAWING A WINTER WASTELAND

sifting the sand

CARVING THE ROCK

the water

IN THE END

MOVING THE MOUNTAIN

Last spring I helped a friend on Galiano Island clear a trail along the top of a cliff that looked out over the waters of Trincomali Channel, facing Vancouver Island. The trail was a challenge, winding up and down, over rock masses and around pine and oak and arbutus trees. We chopped away

TAMING THE WILDERNESS

deadfalls, rooted up Scotch broom (an overseas invader that chokes off native species), broke off dead branches, and hacked away at vines and thorny blackberry bushes. After an hour of strenuous effort I straightened up, panting, and asked him, "Do you think it's *right* for us to tame the wilderness?"

I wasn't trying to get out of a job. I really wondered about Adam's assigned task in Eden, "to subdue the earth, and have dominion over it…to cultivate it and keep it," and of our human tendency ever since to domesticate flora and fauna, to groom and "beautify" our environment wherever we happen to be set down in the vast wildness of our earth's surface. Is this impulse a part of the image of God that remains in us—to bring order out of chaos?

The problems, of course, came with the Fall of Adam and Eve—their independence, their lust for the forbidden. When they were expelled from the Garden and punished, the whole of the created universe was affected. God told them, "Cursed is the ground because of you; through painful toil shall you eat of it…It will produce thorns and thistles for you." I have

questions like, "What does it mean to *subdue* the earth?" or "Were there thistles and thorns before the Fall?" or "Do cycles of decay follow growth as part of God's original plan for life, or is death, the result of decay, a consequence of human disobedience?"

My friend and I tentatively concluded that some plants (like some animals and some people) are wilder than others, harder to control. The fast-growing blackberries and broom are prickly and invasive, while the bunchberries and bracken and trilliums and sedum stay in their place and look charming. Some mushrooms are deadly, others edible. Crabgrass and dandelions take over our lawns while creeping bent is docile, smooth, and velvety in its assigned space. My friend quoted Martin Heidegger, saying that language (and life) are a matter of "clearing a way into being." Today, perhaps, our task is to open up the beauty of God's creation, to clear trails into the wilderness without destroying it, to find a balance between taming the wilderness and allowing it the freedom to be beautifully wild, showing the complexity and originality of the Creation and the Creator.

Oh let the earth

bless the Lord;

O all ye wild, green things

upon the earth, bless ye the Lord,

Praise him and magnify him forever!

Benedicite!

Anglican antiphon

IF YOU CARE FOR ME

speak to me without words
in a spiral of starlings
thrown into a bank of wind, scarves
of an invisible dancer
making the sky a stage.

Make a negligent gesture like the drop
of a chestnut at my feet, the glossy nucleus bounding
out of its spiky casing, rolling to me, a gift
round and brown as a chocolate cream.

Caress me with a curtain of dew
on my moonlit skylight, or boulders shining under
their clear skin of rain. In the rock garden
a crimson cosmos articulates its bright, small world.

Speak to my eyes in syllables of light
and color, if you care for me.

Remind me about space as I watch the finches
peck at the wind in the balsams. The doe
cleaves the air current over
the ribbon of creek. The great blue heron
elbows its way up through gaps wild with branches
and you are opening for me, too,
a new passage between the trees.

By the way you breathe dead leaves
into a small whirlwind of fire
show me, if you care for me, how you can
lift me from the dust, light me like tinder.

The whole universe is the manuscript in which the Creator has written his character and signed his name

We are the beneficiaries of God's two ways of revealing himself: his special revelation, through Scripture and Jesus Christ, show us how God looks and acts; his general revelation is the whole universe, the manuscript in which the Creator has written his character and signed his name.

So I take comfort not just from the words on a page but also from a different message—the images I see written on the sky, the configurations of a flock of birds, the gift of a glossy chestnut. In dew, rocks, rain, flowers, finches I see divine "syllables of light and color" that say, "I care for you." The deer and the great blue heron, daily visitors to my woodland home, remind me of how wild things find their way through the wilderness, as I do, guided by God.

Most of all, I want to be lit like a burning bush, to blaze and shine. I see myself in the leaf fires of autumn and am lifted in the dancing flame.

We say "I care about you" to someone for whom we have deep personal affection. We "care for" someone for whom we are lovingly responsible. In both these senses God has promised to be my Caretaker.

Rest all your cares on him...

he does care for you.

1 PETER 5:7, author's paraphrase

**NEW BIRTH:
HEART SPRING**

*often after easter
last summer's deep
seeds rebel
at their long frozen sleep
split, swell
in the dark under
ground, twist, dance to a new beat
push through a lace of old
pale roots*

*invited by an unseen heat
they spearhead up, almost
as if, suddenly
their tender shoots
find the loam light as air
not dense, not sodden cold...*

*such swift greening of leaf wings
and stalks and pods
is clear celebration
of all sweet springs
combined
of sungold
smell of freshness, wind
first-time felt
light lifting, all new things
all things good and right
and all the old left behind.*

The best fertilizer is the shadow of the gardener.

Spanish proverb

A garden is a place of resurrection
GOD AND HIS FAMILY
WORK TOGETHER THERE TO MAKE IT HAPPEN

When my daughter Robin and her husband, Mark, bought their old house, they not only renovated it into a charming dwelling place but transformed a dingy, blackberry-ridden rectangle behind the house into a place of order, color, and growth. Grass filled the center, and along one edge five-year-old Lindsay scattered wildflower seeds. Perennials grew under the edge of an old barn, and the herb garden, divided into neat, bricked squares, grew garlic and onions and tomatoes and squash. Along the fence peas hung their white flowers and green vertical pods. After the chilly rain and sleet of winter, a garden is a place of resurrection. God and his family work together to make it happen.

In late spring Lindsay and I were picking new peas for dinner: "Grammy, is this pod big enough?" "Well, it's really too big. The peas inside will be tough and bitter." "How about this one?" "Yes, that one's *just right*." Once we had a mound of *just right* pods in our basket, we shelled the peas, glistening, into a pan, one by one, like words in a sentence. We'd split the pods lengthwise to reveal the row of pale green pearls, like tiny eggs, all the time stealing and snacking on their sweet crunch and tang. Big and little fingers flew, jostling the peas out of their mother-grooves, clinking them into the metal pan where, mixed and unmatched, heterogenous, they became "green peas" for dinner—a fresh, green poem to the tongue, better than any prosaic can or frozen vegetable package.

95

SECTION FOUR

I sing God's presence at the birth in Bethlehem's dark night;
Christ living, dying, rising, turns my darkness into light.
Present thou art in bread and wine, Lord. Now thy grace impart
And by thy Holy Spirit's power, be present in my heart.

JUDAS, PETER

because we are all
    but if we find grace
betrayers, taking
    to weep and wait
silver and eating
    after the voice of morning
body and blood and asking
    has crowed in our ears
(guilty) is it I and hearing
    clearly enough
him say yes
    to break our hearts
it would be simple for us all
    he will be there
to rush out
    to ask us each again
and hang ourselves
    do you love me

In the New Testament we are shown pictures of two people—Judas and Peter—who were failures at critical points in their lives. One merely failed. The other learned the singular lesson of how to fail successfully.

The relationship of Master and follower has never been an easy one. To be a Christ-follower means to give up one's independence, to choose rather to listen and obey and learn, to repattern one's thinking, to put the Leader first in such a radical way that by comparison the claims of family, friends, reputation, and possessions grow shadowy and insubstantial.

A disciple cannot use a special relationship to the Leader to win political favors or make money on the side. Somehow, Judas never saw this. Or if he did, he could never divest himself of his not-so-secret love of silver and the power it brings. Perhaps when Jesus said, with quiet emphasis, "You cannot serve God and Mammon," it was Judas whom he looked in the eye. For all his easy piety about giving to the poor Judas had a miserly spirit devoid of real love. In betraying Christ with that false kiss in the midnight Garden for thirty silver coins, he ended up betraying himself.

Peter, on the other hand, lived hard and loved hard. He was pigheaded, impulsive, short-fused, talkative, and often dead wrong. But he was wholehearted. That saved him in the end, after his miserable mistake of fearing to acknowledge his relationship to the fettered Criminal in the center of the courtyard and of not wanting to look like a fool in front of the high priest's servants. He learned, the hard way, that not being willing to look like a fool may be the most foolish attitude of all.

But his strong love for Jesus produced in him equally strong shame when he recognized his failure for what it was—not just betrayal but *denial* of his Master. He saw the truth about himself, and rather than deny his denial, he cried. Peter's kind of crying is the secret to failing successfully. It comes when the truth penetrates our hearts. It signals light breaking—a new day, a fresh chance to find the healing of forgiveness, of saying yes to a voice that asks with gentle persistence, "Do you love me?"

A broken spirit and a tender heart You will never despise, O Lord.

PSALM 51:17, author's paraphrase

Until five years ago in the emergency room of our local hospital, I had never seen blood for what it is. Earlier that day I'd gone bicycling with Kristin, my teenage daughter. Coasting along down a hill on a fresh autumn evening, not paying close attention to what I was doing, my front wheel had accidentally touched her rear wheel. It sent me off balance, spilling me over the handlebars onto the rough country road, scraping the skin off my forehead, nose, chin, hands, and knees. I must have looked appalling, with blood flowing freely and my scraped skin bruised and swelling fast. As soon as Kris saw that I was reviving, she sped off on her bike for help.

Twenty minutes later, rescued by my husband in our station wagon and trundled off to our local hospital, I was finally paying attention to my surroundings. And I realized with astonished empathy that every other patient in the unit was also bleeding.

Blood, a startling color, not the kind of evidence you can ignore, is designed to be almost invisible, doing its essential work unheralded and unseen within the body, hidden, protected within the water-tight envelope of human tissue and skin. Nearly always the red of blood is a signal that something is wrong, that there's a breach in the system.

The incident stayed with me, sinking in, moving deeper from body to mind to heart, reminding me of another event when blood had flowed, a blood that from the foundations of the world was destined by God to be spilled, to be clearly evident to a watching world, to signal both death and life.

TRAUMA UNIT

It was never meant
to burst from the body
so fiercely, to pour unchanneled
from the five wounds
and the unbandaged brow,
drowning the dark wood,
staining the stones
and the gravel below,
clotting in the air
dark with God's absence.

It was created for
a closed system—the unbroken
rhythms of human blood
binding the body of God,

circulating hot, brilliant,
saline, without interruption
between heart, lungs,
and all cells.

But because he was once
emptied, I am each day refilled;
my spirit-arteries
pulse with the vital red
of love; poured out,

The life of

every living thing

is in the blood...

Blood, which is life,

takes away sin.

LEVITICUS 17:11 TEV

it is his life
that now pumps through
my own heart's core. He fled and died
and I have been transfused

We are a church group on our own pilgrimage, touring in Israel, walking where Jesus walked. But we find the barriers of centuries distracting. What I want to see is like the slide projector dissolve that seamlessly replaces one picture with another on the screen. I want to watch as the older images of The Holy Land, imagined since childhood, are replaced with Israel as it is today, the real thing—the shapes of mountain and shore, the taste of grapes and figs and honey and almonds, sycamore trees, fishing boats, shepherds, flocks of sheep and goats, sun rising over Gennesaret. I want to see Christ, not gilded and haloed, peering from some dark interior monument or in chipped mosaic fragments on a wall, but walking with dusty feet like that bedouin man over there.

All these holy sites that we have been visiting are places where once God touched down or scorched the ground with his fiery self or spoke words that changed everything. Believers, far off in time from the primary event, grab and try to protect and seal off these evidences of God's visitation for themselves and their children, until the real stones and the plain solid earth are quite hidden under the accumulation of tawdry human art and artifacts.

Even when we dig down to the original levels (ancient mosaic floors, retaining walls, steps, paving stones), they are lit with dusty wax candles and hung with rotting tapestries. Worse, the "holy sites" are railed off or plastic-coated or plastered with explanatory signs in English and Hebrew and Arabic lending them a kind of artificiality, like specimens in a museum.

The attempt to enrich and make holy the original seems to impoverish it—robbing it of its primitive immediacy and accessibility. The simple and significant turn "traditional" until we can no longer erase time and its dusty layers. We need heaven to break through to us again, primal and forceful and fearful and loving. But Jesus doesn't live here any more, does he? How, here in the flesh, can we see him as he was, as he is?

SLIDE PHOTOGRAPHY:
CLIMBING THE MOUNT OF OLIVES

A gray wall fills the lens—old limestone
crowned with a branching weed
that blocks the early sun (miraculous
that herbs so small can stop
the sun). Hugging the barrier, close
as a disciple, the steep path
creeps up from Gethsemane. The click
and the click of the defining shutter
frames rectangles from which all sounds will die,
carried away by air and time. Like words on the page,
slides are silent. It is the remembering
mind that hears the Arab
children's cries,

crowds ancient alleys with movement and the
pungent smell of sesame oil, recalls a vacant lot
rank with poppies red as
spilled blood.

So how may we, his distant pilgrims,
know him real (whose Garden presence still guards
the gnarled, secret olives)? Faith
listens for his story in the everyday
neigh of a donkey, an explosive obscenity,
the threat of armed soldiers, sweat
on any dark skin, the clink of coins,
thorns pricking, metal clanging on metal,
a cloth tearing.

Faith is a certain widening of the imagination

L.S.

103

PRESENTS

What's as good as getting?
The anticipation, snow
in the air, people with lists,
voices that drop when you
enter the room, the pine-wood
fire smell, and the smell of pine
needles on the trimmed tree
by the window—it all
narrows down
to the heft of the package
in the hands, the wondering,
the unwrapping (carefully—
the paper too pretty
to tear), the Oh! the Ah! What's
as good as getting

if not giving?
The covert questions, the catalogs
with corners turned back,
the love that overlooks cost,
the hiding place
in the hamper, the card whose
colored words can't say it all,
the glee of linking want/wish
with have/hold, the handing over,
fingers brushing, the thing
disclosed at last, the spark
as the eyes meet,
and the hug. What's
as good as giving?

GETTING AND GIVING

Christmas is the time of gifts. But have you noticed how much the advertising of consumer goods plays on our most selfish and materialistic impulses? Rather than being told to give generously to others, we hear "Be good to yourself," "Live a little," "You *deserve* it!" By such maxims we all too easily rationalize our own Yuletide self-indulgence.

In a "give me" age, things that once had to be earned are now expected as "our rights." People once honored and valued are taken for granted. Self-ism has become the new idolatry, and "I'm *worth* it" the new rule of thumb. Material values have risen to the top rung of the ladder, and anything we cannot see and touch and prove and *use* is discounted as irrelevant; spiritual realities are dismissed as impractical and insignificant in an age of upward mobility.

How refreshing it is, in this context, to think of the downward mobility of Jesus, who left behind the riches of heaven, stripped himself of kingly splendor, was willing to be as poor and abused and out of step with his age as the most threadbare beggar he reached down and touched with the gift of love and healing. Jesus said, "It is better to give than to receive," and proved that he meant it when he gave his life away to us.

Thanks be to God for his indescribable Gift

2 CORINTHIANS 9:15 NIV

SUDDEN VALLEY ROAD

DEATH HERE
AUTO ACCIDENT
FRIDAY, APRIL 1

It stares at me as if
I did it—the cardboard sign, fogwarped,
stained by the steady grief of rain.
Nailed to a phone pole beside the
rising slick of the road, the black letters
signal something too huge to say. Like a white
flag that stands for a whole army
in surrender, its skewed rectangle shrinks
the truth, forces me to fill the details in
as I bank on the steep curve,
tires skidding. I feel it
all the way down the other side—
how it would be to lie there,
spilled along the gravel, body
ragged as the red leaves bleeding
around the bend, eyes milky
under the shroud that fogs the mountain.

Somehow the notice is fastened
to a death that still
shudders around the curving world
whose naked placard, tacked to a post
on the brow of a skull-shaped hill
affronts all of us fools,
through the drizzle of years,
as though we did it.

GOOD FRIDAY

Sudden Valley Road is a steep highway that curves up out of the valley where I live in the waning months of the year, in the wooded foothills of the Cascade Mountains of Washington State, an area known for its beauty, its rain, and its fog. I drove that road every day, and every day at a certain point near the summit I was faced with a roughly lettered cardboard sign tacked to a telephone pole. It proclaimed a death by accident earlier that year—ironically, on April Fools' Day.

The sign had a powerful impact on me. I sensed that it was drawing me into a new understanding of violent death and, in particular, of the long-ago death on the cross in which, somehow, *I* had participated.

To the marrow of my bones I *felt* death from two angles. First I imagined my way into what it would be like to die as that drunken driver had died, my car going out of control in the dark of a rainy night and smashing into the telephone pole. I could almost hear the squeal of brakes and the sound of metal crumpling. I could feel the shocking impact, the violence as my battered body flew through the windshield and landed on the rough gravel. I could hear the deathlike silence afterwards, when the only sound was the spit of rain on the ground.

And then in a different way I felt the reality of death, another death. This sodden sign reminded me of the sign nailed to Jesus' cross. *That* death was not an accident. It was ordained from before the beginning of time, but that absolved no one from blame. And the knowledge drove into me like an iron spike that I was one of the fools who had nailed him, and can still nail him, to the cross by my indifference to who he really is. That I still have autonomy, and the option of saying, in my casual self-will and independence, "Away with him, I will not have this man to be king over me."

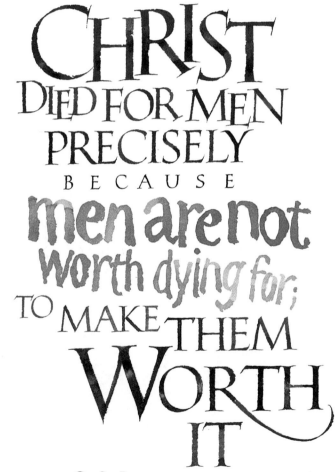

CHRIST DIED FOR MEN PRECISELY BECAUSE men are not worth dying for; TO MAKE THEM WORTH IT

C. S. Lewis
in *The World's Last Night*

HE was a plain man
and learned no LATIN
Having left all gold behind
he dealt out peace
to all us wild ones
and the weather
He ate fish, bread,
country wine and GOD's WILL
Dust sandalled his feet
He wore purple only once
and that was an irony

Jesus contradicted all their presuppositions.

They were looking for a warrior king, with political and military power, a leader who would free them from the iron rule of Rome. Jesus was indeed born into the kingly line of Judah, but rather than leading the people into battle he told them to love their enemies and forgive the wrongs done to them. He told them: "Blessed are the meek, the merciful, the peacemakers," and he gave them himself as their prime example. He had no army; his following was a ragged bunch of fishermen and a few women, and his kingdom a secret one. Instead of publicizing his power, he worked underground. "Don't tell," he'd say to a healed leper.

They wanted a figurehead, dominant, educated, handsome, autocratic, magnetic, one who could give them again a sense of national pride. Jesus was strong but humble, wise but simple. Though he was decisive his decisions ran counter to popular opinion. He gave his listeners *radical* instructions—"Give away your shirt...." "When you're hit, turn your other cheek for another blow..." "Be happy when you are persecuted..."

"Don't worry so much about eating and drinking and what you wear..."

They wanted a man of action, a messianic figure who would effect major changes in their world. Jesus talked of small but potent things— salt, a mustard seed, yeast, a coin, a pearl, a cup of cold water. He spoke of quiet realities—light, and water, and narrow roads, and shepherds. He taught his followers to be seed scatterers, dough-kneaders, light-bearers.

They wanted a monarch in a grand palace, eating and dressing extravagantly, holding court surrounded by nobles, with stables full of horses and chariots. But Jesus wandered by foot from place to place, without a home to call his own. The only time he was called a king and wore a robe to match was at his own trial. It was done in mockery; everyone thought the whole thing a farce.

They didn't see what was going on because they were searching for something superficial and transient. Jesus, who really was royal, invaded the heart and revolutionized what went on *inside* people—a change that would be forever, outlasting all earthly kings and kingdoms.

Not by might, nor by power,

but by my spirit,

says the LORD *of hosts.*

ZECHARIAH 4:6 NRSV

Two things seem to be necessary for the moment of recognition to flash between Jesus and us. The prerequisites were exemplified on the road to Emmaus after Jesus' death, when his two downcast friends (who may have been husband and wife) were trying to cope with their bewilderment that he was gone.

And Jesus came and walked beside them. He took the initiative. Jesus' questions to them—"What are you so concerned about?" and "What things?" —were asked not out of his ignorance but to help these two to talk with him, to open up their amazement and grief to him, to let him set things in order in their minds and hearts. (And he invites us to enter the same kind of conversation with him until our hearts "burn within us.")

But it was in the context of even greater intimacy, at the evening meal, as he blessed and broke the bread for them, that "their eyes were opened and they recognized him." This couldn't have happened unless their eyes were pure, unless they wanted with all their hearts to see him.

Today it is the same. Jesus takes the lovely initiative with us. By his Spirit he comes to us out of the text of Scripture. And then, in the intimacy of communion, if our eyes are pure, comes the moment of recognition. We look back into his eyes and see God.

FOR THEY SHALL SEE GOD

They only saw Jesus—and then but the outside Jesus,
or a little more. They were not pure in heart....
They saw Him with their eyes, but not
with those eyes which alone can see God....
the thought-eyes, the truth-eyes,
the love-eyes can see Him.
George MacDonald

Christ risen was rarely
recognized by sight.
They had to get beyond the way he looked.
Evidence stronger than
his voice and face and footstep
waited to grow in them, to guide
their groping from despair,
their stretching toward belief.

We are as blind as they
until the opening of our deeper eyes
shows us the hands that bless
and break our bread,
until we finger
wounds that tell our healing
or witness a miracle of fish,
dawn-caught after our long night
of empty nets.
Handling his Word, we feel his flesh,
his bones, and hear his voice
calling our early-morning name

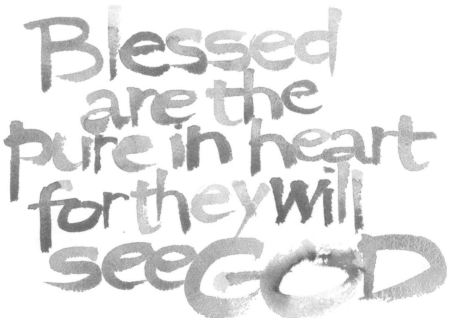

MATTHEW 5:8 NIV

STEP ON IT

All these broken bridges—
we have always tried to build them
to each other and to heaven.
Why is it such a sad surprise
when last year's iron-strong,
out-thrust organization, this month's
shining project, today's
far-flung silver network
of good resolutions
all answer the future's questions with
rust, and the sharp, ugly jutting
of the unfinished?
We have miscalculated every time.
Our blueprints are smudged.
We never order enough steel.
Our foundations are shallow as mud.
Our cables fray.
Our superstructure is stuck together
clumsily, with rivets of the wrong size.

We are our own botched bridges.
We were schooled in Babel
and our ambitious soaring sinks
in the sea. How could we hope to carry
your heavy glory? We cannot even bear
the weight of our own failure.

But you did the unthinkable.
You built one bridge to us
solid enough, long enough, strong enough
to stand all tides for all time, linking
the unlinkable.

THE BRIDGE

There is always a gap between present reality and future potential.

A gift unwrapped has never been truly received. An uncashed check cannot be spent. A bridge that spans a raging river is useless to us unless we begin to advance across it.

The divide between earth and heaven, between us and God, is one that only Jesus Christ could reconnect. He is our link to life and eternity—a bridge to be stepped onto so that it bears our whole weight as we cross the space from one side to the other.

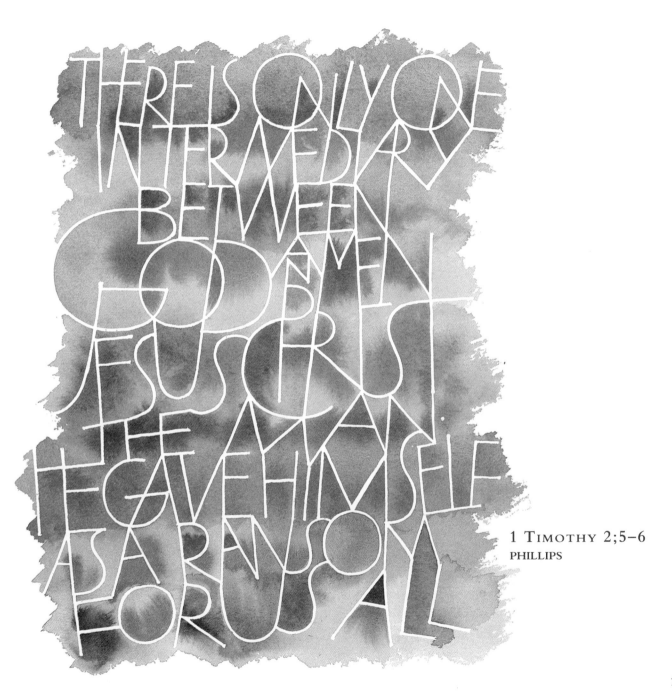

THERE IS ONLY ONE INTERMEDIARY BETWEEN GOD & MEN JESUS CHRIST THE MAN HE GAVE HIMSELF AS A RANSOM FOR US ALL

1 TIMOTHY 2;5–6
PHILLIPS

113

MARY'S SONG

Blue homespun and the bend of my breast
keep warm this small hot naked star
fallen to my arms. (Rest...
you who have had so far
to come.) Now nearness satisfies
the body of God sweetly.
Quiet he lies, whose vigor
hurled a universe. He sleeps
whose eyelids have not closed before.

His breath (so slight
it seems no breath at all) once ruffled
the dark deeps
to sprout a world.
Charmed by doves' voices, the whisper
of straw, he dreams,
hearing no music from his other spheres.
Breath, mouth, ears, eyes,
he is curtailed
who overflowed all skies,
all years.
Older than eternity, now he
is new. Now native to earth as I am, nailed
to my poor planet,
caught that I might be free,
blind in my womb to know my darkness ended,
brought to this birth
for me to be new-born,
and for him to see me mended,
I must see him torn.

*Because
eternity
was closeted
in time
He is
our
open door
to forever*

"Made Flesh" by LUCI SHAW

We often think of Jesus' suffering on this earth. Sometimes we forget that most of what we know about Mary, Jesus' mother, is also in the context of pain. Even her name means "bitter."

Her role was a difficult one from the start. Young and inexperienced, she was called by the Lord's angel to a pregnancy that owned no human father and opened her to charges of promiscuity. Her vocation was to be the mother of a paradox—God in a man's body, a man who would be considered a failed rebel by the leaders in his day, and finally a criminal.

Early on, she felt dismay at having to travel to Bethlehem in her ninth month, of giving birth in the most primitive and comfortless of conditions, of knowing later that her own little one survived at the life cost of Bethlehem's baby boys who were slaughtered by Herod in Jesus' place.

On the eighth day after Jesus' birth a prophecy laced with further torment was spoken to Mary: "A sword will pierce your own soul"—a pain for her to ponder and dread for over thirty years. During that waiting time, Jesus directed some of his hardest sayings to his gentle mother—words that must have wounded. But the culmination of all her anguish was at the cross, under its very arm, as she watched her beloved son die a slow and brutal death.

But hers was not the kind of dead-end pain that has no meaning. She was privileged to be caught up in the life of the One who fought the fierce battle between light and darkness. We can understand that mix of pain and joy only as we carry Christ in our hearts, birthing him into a hostile world. That may mean suffering; we may be as misunderstood as Mary. But there is a reward: *Because eternity was closeted in time, he is our open door to forever.*

driving: Bach
at work on FM
his final voice unfaltering
cut off mid-
phrase

through the windshield
plays the blue
orchestra of sky

the finale is flying
flying
up there, still
soli gloria deo

hope redeems
my earthbound progress: I
shall hear Bach whole
and sing with him
the new song
the infinite fugue
he is working on

RAPTURE

He who began a good work in you will carry it on to

FINISHING THE UNFINISHED

Driving one day, I was listening to classical music on our local classical music station. The announcer prefaced the playing of a baroque fugue by telling us that Johann Sebastian Bach had scored a set of eighteen pieces entitled "The Art of Fugue." As was Bach's habit, he had written on the scores *"soli gloria deo"*—glory to God alone.

What riveted my attention was that quite unexpectedly, during the playing of the final Fugue no. 18, the harpsichord stopped in the middle of an unresolved chord. It was the moment of sudden death and farewell and relinquishment for Bach—the moment of his rapture. The effect of the notes left resonating in the air was so poignant for me, so full of surprise and pain, like a promise half-spoken, that my eyes filled with sudden tears and I had to pull off to the shoulder of the road.

Until I realized—heaven is full of music. Bach must feel perfectly at home there. He is probably writing cantatas and oratorios for angels and must long ago have finished Fugue no. 18.

I can hardly wait to hear how it ends.

COMPLETION

PHILIPPIANS 1:6 NIV

CHANCE

Did God take his chances
on a son sent to fill flesh?
Was metamorphosis a divine risk?

Once embodied
might he not find
earth's poignancies too sharp,
sweet flesh too sweet to discard?
Might not human joys
(the growing
of body, mind, and will,
knowing
companionship,
the taste of shared bread,
the smell of olives,
new-carved cedar-wood, and wine,
morning's chill
on a bare head,
rough, warm wool,

a near, dust-blue Judean hill,
evening's shine
of oil lamps through an
open door,
day's work, tired muscles,
a bed on the floor)
make up for the limitations?
Might he not even wish
for a peaceful death from old age?

Ah, Father, but you knew
the Incarnation was no gamble!
We are the risk you run.
Our destiny is not so clearly defined.
It's either/or for us.

And when I say you took no chance on him,
he being our one chance of heaven,
I mean, rather,
once chosen, he's no chance
but certainty.

It's always tempting to ask the "What if?" questions: What if Eve had not given in to the serpent's temptation?" or "What if Noah's ark had sunk, with all its occupants?" or "What if Moses had lacked the courage to lead the Israelites across the Red Sea?" and the most significant question of all: "What if Jesus had found human life so satisfying that he abandoned his Father's plan and turned away from the cross?"

We can speculate as much as we want, but the fact is that all those choices were made as the Bible records them. And because Jesus did "set his face toward Jerusalem," we can now set our faces toward heaven with the certainty of reaching it. For us there's no "What if?"

Pleased as man with man to dwell Jesus, our Emanuel

"Hark! The Herald Angels Sing" by CHARLES WESLEY

THE PARTAKING

*Bread of the Presence was in Moses' day
served on engraved gold plates
to you and your select few.
And in exclusive glory
one alone and lonely priest
sprinkled with fear
the ceremonial drops that pleaded
failure for another year
to you, known then as only high and holy—
heavens apart from the common crowd.*

*Often we taste the granular body of wheat
(Think of the Grain that died!)
and swallow together
the grape's warm, bitter blood
(Remember First Fruit)
knowing ourselves a part of you
as you took part of us,
flowed in our kind of veins,
quickened cells like ours
into a human subdividing.
Now you are multiplied—we are your fingers
and your feet, your tender heart—
we are your broken side.*

*Take now and crumble small and
scatter us—food for the world—
your contemporary shewbread.
Feed us to more than five thousand,
and in our dark, daily flood of living
pour yourself out again!*

Around the world, at every stage of history, humans have needed two essentials for survival—*food* and *drink*.

At the end of his earthly ministry Jesus ate a meal with his friends. Because he wanted them to go on remembering him, he gave them two pictures of himself—*bread* and *wine*—basic food and drink that can be found in any culture. He linked the bread and wine to his own body and blood in a unique way. Holding out the cup of wine and the loaf of bread, he said, "This is my body. This is my blood."

Ask yourself, How is bread like Jesus' human body (solid like flesh, ground from grain and baked to picture his suffering for us, textured, cellular)? And how is wine like Jesus' human blood (fluid, red, made from crushed grapes)?

Jesus also said, "Do this...until I come again." He wanted them, and us, to enact this picture of his enfleshment, his being born human—flesh and blood like you and me so that he can relate to us and we to him.

Paul tells us that we are now Christ's body. That means that we can be the *fingers* of Jesus, touching others in love and healing; his *feet*, going where he would have gone; his *voice*, saying his words to people who need to hear from God; his *eyes*, looking with compassion and discernment into the eyes of others; his Shepherd *arms*, carrying home lost lambs. We are even the wounded *side* of Jesus, feeling some of his brokenness, and that of the world.

As we take the communion bread and wine into our mouths, these elements can picture not only Jesus but what he wants us to be—his body and blood broken and poured out for the needs of the world.

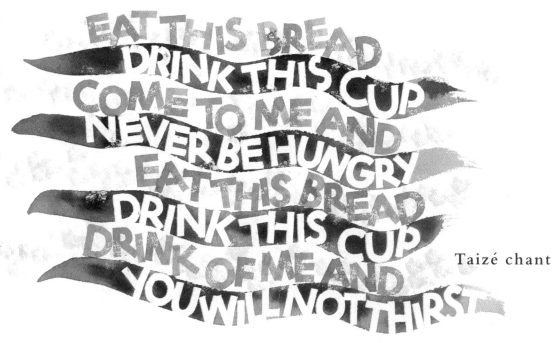

EAT THIS BREAD
DRINK THIS CUP
COME TO ME AND
NEVER BE HUNGRY
EAT THIS BREAD
DRINK THIS CUP
DRINK OF ME AND
YOU WILL NOT THIRST

Taizé chant

CRAFTSMAN

Carpenter's son, carpenter's son,
is the wood fine
and smoothly sanded, or rough-grained,
lying along your back? Was it well-planed?
did they use
a plumbline
When they set you up? Is the angle true?
Why did they choose
that dark, expensive stain
to gloss the timbers
next to your feet and fingers? You
should know—who,
Joseph-trained, judged all trees
for special service.
Carpenter's son, carpenter's son,
Were the nails new and cleanly driven
when the dark hammers sang?
Is the earth warped from where you hang,
high enough for a
world view?
Carpenter's son, carpenter's son,
was it a job well done?

Think of it—Jesus, Creator of the universe, grew up to be a small-town carpenter, moving from the macrocosm to the microcosm. But he continued to be a *maker* who shaped and crafted raw materials into usefulness and beauty, trained by his human father, Joseph, a skilled carpenter.

We can be sure that in Jesus' careful hands the yokes he carved and sanded were comfortable around the necks of farm animals, that the doors and doorframes he planed and hung were solid and square, as were his tables and boxes and shelves. And his scythe handles didn't blister the farmers' hands with rough spots; his carpentry jobs were always well done.

When he was hung, at last, on a wooden cross made by some other carpenter, he must have judged its workmanship. As to the nailing of his hands and feet to that wood—we must ask of God, was it "a job well-done"?

It was all too well-done. The cross didn't crack under his weight, and the nails didn't pull out. But the craftsmanship of the job made all the difference in the world to us. His dying, on a carpentered cross, now means our living forever.

Jesus, Jesus, carpenter of Nazareth,

can you make a lintel? Can you make a door?

Jesus, Jesus, carpenter of Nazareth,

Can you make a universe where there was none before?

Jesus, Jesus, carpenter of Nazareth,

Living in the midst of us, a working man, and poor,

How shall we esteem you, holy, humble carpenter?

By the universe you made—and also, by the door.

ELIZABETH ROONEY in *A Widening Light*

**THE
FOOLISHNESS
OF GOD**

*Perform impossibilities
or perish. Thrust out now
the unseasonal ripe figs
among your leaves. Expect
the mountain to be moved.
Hate parents, friends, and all
materiality. Love every enemy.
Forgive more times than seventy-
seven. Camel-like, squeeze by
into the kingdom through
the needle's eye. All fear quell.
Hack off your hand, or else,
unbloodied, go to hell.*

*Thus the divine unreason.
Despairing now, you cry
with earthy logic—How?
And I, your God, reply:
Leap from your weedy shallows.
Dive into the moving water.
Eyeless, learn to see
truly. Find in my folly your
true sanity. Then, Spirit-driven,
run on my narrow way, sure
as a child. Probe, hold
my unhealed hand, and
bloody, enter heaven.*

The sermon was about a fig tree. The story, as told in the gospel of Mark, describes how Jesus, hungry, went up to a leafy fig tree to find some fruit to eat. When he saw that it was barren of figs, he cursed it. By the next day it had withered from the roots up. The surprising thing is that Jesus' demand for figs seems so unreasonable. As the gospel narrative makes clear, "It was not the season for figs." How, then, could Jesus *expect* to find fruit on it?

Sometimes God's demands on us seem unreasonable. "After all," we protest, "we're only human." Where can we find the faith to move mountains? How can he ask us to "hate" our parents? Must we actually love our enemies? Or forgive and forgive and forgive, more than four hundred ninety times? Or give the shirt off our backs to some panhandler? Does God really expect us to pluck out our eyeballs or hack off our hands if they "offend" us?

These and other divine requirements are sometimes known as "the hard sayings of Jesus." But our response to God's desire for our perfection is too often based on human logic. No. We cannot possibly live up to his standards; we are flawed, foolish, inadequate. Only as we plunge into the supernatural realms of the Spirit, forsaking the weedy shallows of our human wisdom, can we see that God's "foolishness" is really his super-wisdom. "My ways are not your ways," he tells us, "nor are your thoughts my thoughts." If we are to see from God's perspective, we must allow the Holy Spirit to "lead us into truth." Only then will we be able to "perform impossibilities."

THE FOOLISHNESS OF GOD IS WISER THAN MAN'S WISDOM

1 CORINTHIANS 1:25 NIV

TO KNOW HIM RISEN

Is it obliquely
through time's telescope, thick-
lensed with two thousand Easters?

Or to my ear in Latin, three chanted
"Kyries" triumphing over a purple chancel?
Or in a rectangular glance at sepia postcards
of Jerusalem's Historic Sites?
Can I touch him through the cliché crust
of lilies, stained glass, sunrise services?
Is a symbol soluble?
Can I flush out my eyes and rinse away
the scales?
Must I be there?

Must I feel his freshness
at an interval of inches? and sense,
incredulous, the reassurance of warm breath?
and hear again the grit of stone
under his sandal sole?
those familiar Judean vowels
in the deep voicing of beatitude? recognize
the straight stance, quick eye,
strength, purpose, movement, clear command—
all the swift three-day antonyms of death
that spring up to dispel its sting,
to contradict its loss?
Must I be Thomas—belligerent in doubt,
hesitant, tentative, convinced, humbled, loved,
and there?
Must sight sustain belief?
Or is a closer blessedness
to know him risen—now
in this moment's finger-thrust of faith—here
as an inner eyelid lifts?

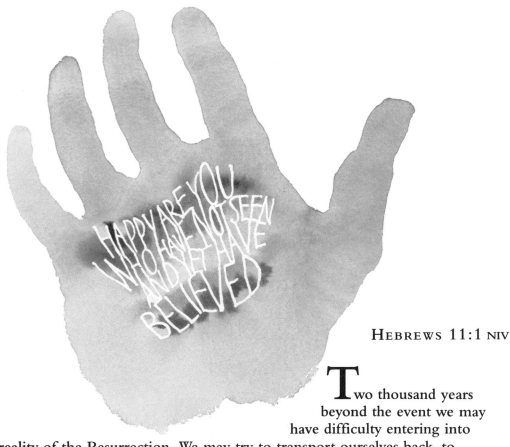

HAPPY ARE YOU WHO HAVE NOT SEEN AND YET HAVE BELIEVED

HEBREWS 11:1 NIV

Two thousand years beyond the event we may have difficulty entering into the reality of the Resurrection. We may try to transport ourselves back, to experience it firsthand, to imagine what it would have been like to cry Peter's tears of remorse or, shaking with fear, to barricade ourselves in the upper room and then see the risen Jesus suddenly *there* with us, without having opened the door. We may even attempt to feel Thomas's uncertainty about Jesus, a skepticism that demanded the proof of touch—his fingers on Jesus' unhealed wounds.

Only by an act of faith may our imaginations be so vitalized that we know deeply that these things did indeed happen and are as important for us, Jesus' followers today, as they were two thousand years back.